Special Force

Navy SEALS

By Eric Z

Eric Z

ISBN: 9798638408213

Which Special Forces Are YOU?

Take the quiz, it's fun and it's free!

How to scan a QR code (Apple)

1. Open the Camera app from the Home screen, Control Center, or Lock screen.
2. Select the rear facing camera. Hold your device so that the QR code appears in the viewfinder in the Camera app. Your device recognizes the QR code and shows a notification.
3. Tap the notification to open the link associated with the QR code.

Android devices:
Download any
"QR Code Reader"
in the play store:

Introduction

If you have ever wondered if the Navy SEALs are the right Special Forces for you, then this book is for YOU!

A word on the term "Special Forces":

In the United States "Special Forces" specifically means the US Army's Special Forces, while the term special operations forces (SOF) is used for the others, like Navy SEALs, Marines Recon etc.

So YES, Navy SEALs are Special Forces, but to be accurate they are Special Operations Forces, whereas the United States Army has the actual branch called "Special Forces" also known as the Green Berets and Army Rangers.

In Europe, and the rest of the world there is no such difference, they are all called "Special Forces".

Joining the Navy

No matter how old you are, your path as a Navy SEAL begins now—as in *right now!*

Even if you are only 12 or 13 years old, you can start on your physical fitness right now, *and you should.*

If you prepare your body before you go to try out for the Navy SEALs, you will have a much better chance of passing their tough physical requirements.

Also, you must "stay clean" because the military does not accept anyone with a criminal record. That means you may NEVER get arrested.The first step in joining the armed forces is going to your recruiter and asking about the Navy SEAL program.

Also, you must definitely ask about a "guaranteed job".

The guaranteed job is the most important thing you must clarify BEFORE joining the armed forces!

Why?

Because If you do not pass the BUDS test for the Navy SEALs, guess what happens? You go back to the "regular" Navy and do your job—the job you chose at the recruiter. If you don't have a guaranteed job, then the Navy will pick one for you!

And that's the problem—that is a very bad idea, because then they will pick something that you probably won't like, for example...a cook!

Remember, roughly 80% of the people who apply to be a Navy SEAL don't make it through BUDs.

So you had better pick something that you would like to do in the Navy, just in case you don't become a Navy SEAL. Because you're going to be in the Navy for a minimum of 4 years regardless of if you pass BUDs *or not*.

And you don't want to join the Navy to be a cook, do you?

So make sure you get a guaranteed job FIRST.

And remember: if your recruiter can't give you a guaranteed job, you don't have to join. This point is so important that I even made a video about it for you:

Before joining the Navy you must take several tests:

You must take the ASVAB—which you can also do in High-School before you even go to the recruiter. The ASVAB is a basic aptitude test that measures reading comprehension, memory retention, logical thinking, and other things, so make sure you study hard and get good grades on this test.

The CSORT - Computerized Special Operations Resiliency Test:

The CSORT is your first introduction to stress and resilience. Something you need a lot of as a Navy SEAL. So the first stress test is—you cannot study for this test!

There are no materials or study guides, and almost no information online, and on top of that you can only take this test once.

You will do this test at your recruiter's office, like the ASVAB, before even being accepted for further tests, and being admitted to the Navy SEALs program.

It is designed to measure your ability to handle stress and it has three main areas:

- Performance strategies
- Psychological resilience
- Personality traits

You can achieve a score from 1 to 4 with 4 being best.

Once you have passed these tests, then you go to MEPS: the Military Entrance Processing Station.

Here you will do more physical screening and this is also where you raise your right hand and take the oath to join the Navy.

Then you are officially in the Navy, and you will now go to the "Pre-BUDs training. This is done at the SEAL school at the Naval Station at Great Lakes Illinois, the actual start of the Navy SEAL program!

For Officers

If you want to be an officer in the Navy, you will have to finish college first, and get your Bachelor's degree. Then you apply for officer candidate school —"OCS".

The wonderful thing about the Navy, and other armed forces, is that they will help you through college, and even pay for some of your college tuition!

This program is called the Naval Reserve Officers Training Corps, or NROTC.

You should talk to your recruiter about NROTC and becoming an officer BEFORE you join, and you will then request the Navy SEALs BUDs training right after OCS.

Be aware that the Navy needs more enlisted SEALs than officer SEALs at a ratio of about 10 to 1.

This means it will be harder for you to become a SEAL, as the selection process is even stricter. You must be accepted by a board of SEAL officers to even start the SEAL training and go to OCS and BUDs.

However, being an officer in the armed forces is ALWAYS better than being enlisted.

An officer has a higher rank and more pay, and is in a position of LEADERSHIP right out of Officer Candidate School. Also, the career opportunities AFTER the Navy are much better.

That's why it's super important to talk to your recruiter if you want to join the Navy SEALs as an officer.

Here's another tip that most people don't think of:

***NEVER* join the military in December!**

What happens is this: Christmas is a federal holiday, so your basic training will not count during Christmas! You'll be "on vacation" in bootcamp, and this vacation time does not count to your basic training. So for one or two weeks you're stuck there, and they don't count, and this LENGTHENS the time you are in basic training. So never join any of the armed forces in December.

Summary - First Steps

1. Go to your nearest recruiter and ask about joining the Navy SEALs program.
2. Get a "GUARANTEED JOB" at the recruiter.
3. Do the ASVAB and CSORT tests, also at the recruiter.
4. Go to MEPS and pass more physical screenings and CONFIRM your guaranteed job!
5. Take the OATH
6. You're in! Off you go to Pre-BUDs training!

HONOR

COURAGE

COMMITMENT

The United States Navy's Core Values!

Training Schedule & Physical Requirements

NAVAL SPECIAL WARFARE PREPARATORY SCHOOL (NSW PREP)

TWO MONTHS

NSW Prep ends with a modified PST which you must pass:

1000-yard swim - with fins (20 minutes or less)
Push-ups: at least 70 (two-minute time limit)
Pull-ups: at least 10 (two-minute time limit)
Curl-ups: at least 60 (two-minute time limit)
Four-mile run - with shoes and pants (31 minutes or under)

First comes the "Pre-BUDs" or Navy SEAL Prep-School.

This school is all about getting you in shape for SEAL school.

Also, this phase is used to test your physical fitness.

Only the toughest candidates pass.

The Navy SEALs have one of the toughest entry requirements of all Special Forces. There is a lot of swimming involved. You have to swim 500 yards in less than 9 minutes with the combat swimmer side stroke and...

- You have to do 80 to 100 push-ups in 1 in 2 minutes
- You have to do 80 to 100 sit-ups in 2 minutes
- 15-20 pull-ups
- And you have to run 1 1/2 miles in 9 minutes in full battle Gear and boots

If you pass this physical test then you get to go to the Navy SEAL School; this is the next phase and is called "BUDs"Basic **U**nderwater **D**emolition **S**eal training.

If you can't make it past this test, then you're removed from the SEAL training pipeline and reclassified into other jobs in the Navy. This is where the **guaranteed job** becomes very important!

The only easy day was yesterday — Navy SEALs Motto

NAVAL SPECIAL WARFARE ORIENTATION

You're finally in BUDs!

Basic Underwater Demolition SEAL Training.

This is where your Navy SEAL training and *testing* really start.

NAVAL SPECIAL WARFARE ORIENTATION (NSWO)

BUD/S Orientation
3 Weeks
Officers and enlisted candidates
hit the obstacle course
get swimming and
learn the values of teamwork
and perseverance

BUDs Training

BUDs training is separated into three different phases:

Phase 1 - Physical Conditioning

Phase 2 - Combat Diving

Phase 3 - Land Warfare

After that comes:
— SEAL Qualification Training

— Maritime Training

— Advanced Weapons Training

In BUD/S training you have a helmet and you have to paint it a new color for each phase of BUD/S.

3 phases = 3 colors:

- **Green-phase 1**
- **Blue-phase 2**
- **Red-phase 3**

Three phases, and each one must be passed...

Phase 1 Physical Conditioning

FIRST PHASE - BASIC CONDITIONING

SEVEN WEEKS + HELL WEEK!

In this phase candidates will build more physical training, water competency and mental tenacity while continuing to build teamwork.
Additionally, the fourth week is...
HELL WEEK!

Phase one is physical conditioning which takes 7 weeks.

In this phase is also the dreaded **"Hell Week".**

This phase is all about mind over body

You have to force yourself to keep going, and the navy instructors will test you, and push you, and do everything to make you give up.

During Hell Week you go for one week without sleep!

During Hell Week you will get a maximum of four hours of sleep, but that's *in the water and mud!* You will be doing all sorts of grueling tasks in the mud and the water, with trainers yelling at you, and simulated warfare, and bombs and flares, and machine guns going off around you the whole time.

It is rumored that they actually use REAL bullets when you are crawling through the trenches and under the barbed wire.

Only the toughest candidates get through this phase. Additionally, only the candidates that band together as a team make it.

This is where a lot of SEAL candidates drop out, about 80%!

As a matter of fact, this is where the famous brass ship's bell is.

In this phase, any candidate can ring the bell, at any time, and leave the training, and give up his goal of being a Navy SEAL.

It's called "Drop On Request." You have to drop your helmet next to the bell, and then ring it three times, and you're out!

Phase 2 Combat Diving

SECOND PHASE - COMBAT DIVING

Seven weeks.
Candidates become basic combat swimmers and learn open and closed-circuit diving

When you are done with Phase 1, you go to Phase 2: COMBAT DIVING.

This is a really technical and challenging phase.

Not only must you master swimming, but all of the tools the Navy SEALs use to breathe underwater.

This is no ordinary swimming school.

In this school, you will be tested and pushed to the limit!

You have to learn to not be afraid of the water: you are thrown into the pool with your hands tied behind your back, and your feet are tied together too!

This is called "drown proofing"...

Navy SEALs "drown proofing" exercise:

Yes, it is possible to *not drown* with your hands and feet tied together in the water, and you must master this as a Navy Seal!

You will also learn to swim underwater for a looong way. Many candidates lose consciousness underwater! The trainers are monitoring them closely and always pull them out of the pool in time. But it is all about MIND OVER BODY. You must push yourself to make it to the other end of the pool, underwater, no matter how bad your lungs are burning and wanting air. It's you against your body!

On top of that, once you do use equipment like rebreathers and fins and masks, your trainer will simulate an attack underwater, and intentionally confuse you, and rip your mask off, and try to foul your oxygen lines. The instructor will actually tie knots in your oxygen Lines!

This stress test is designed to make you handle underwater emergencies. If you can't put your mask back on, and get your gear working, and get the KNOT out of your lines, then you don't pass, and you're taken out of Navy SEAL school.

Later, you will use the more advanced equipment—this is no ordinary "SCUBA" diving.

A normal scuba diving system exhales your breath out into the water, which creates a lot of bubbles, *bubbles that the enemy could see.*

A Navy SEAL combat diver uses special equipment like REBREATHERS so that the enemy can't see the bubbles he exhales—because there are none!

This is vitally important; the Navy Seals rely on stealth to sneak up on the enemy, and insert themselves deep into enemy territory without being detected.

This is also called "closed circuit diving".

It uses a rebreather that fully absorbs the carbon dioxide of your exhaled breath. Your exhaled breath is "scrubbed"—better said, the CO2 is removed, and the oxygen is put back into the system to be breathed again, hence "rebreathing."

The science behind this device is interesting indeed. It is a CHEMICAL PROCESS which removes the carbon dioxide from your exhaled breath, and leaves the oxygen. The carbon dioxide is fully absorbed by several chemicals in the scrubber canister. Most scrubbers contain some form of SODA LIME; a mixture of NaOH (sodium hydroxide) & CaO (calcium oxide) chemicals.

The Draeger Rebreathing System:

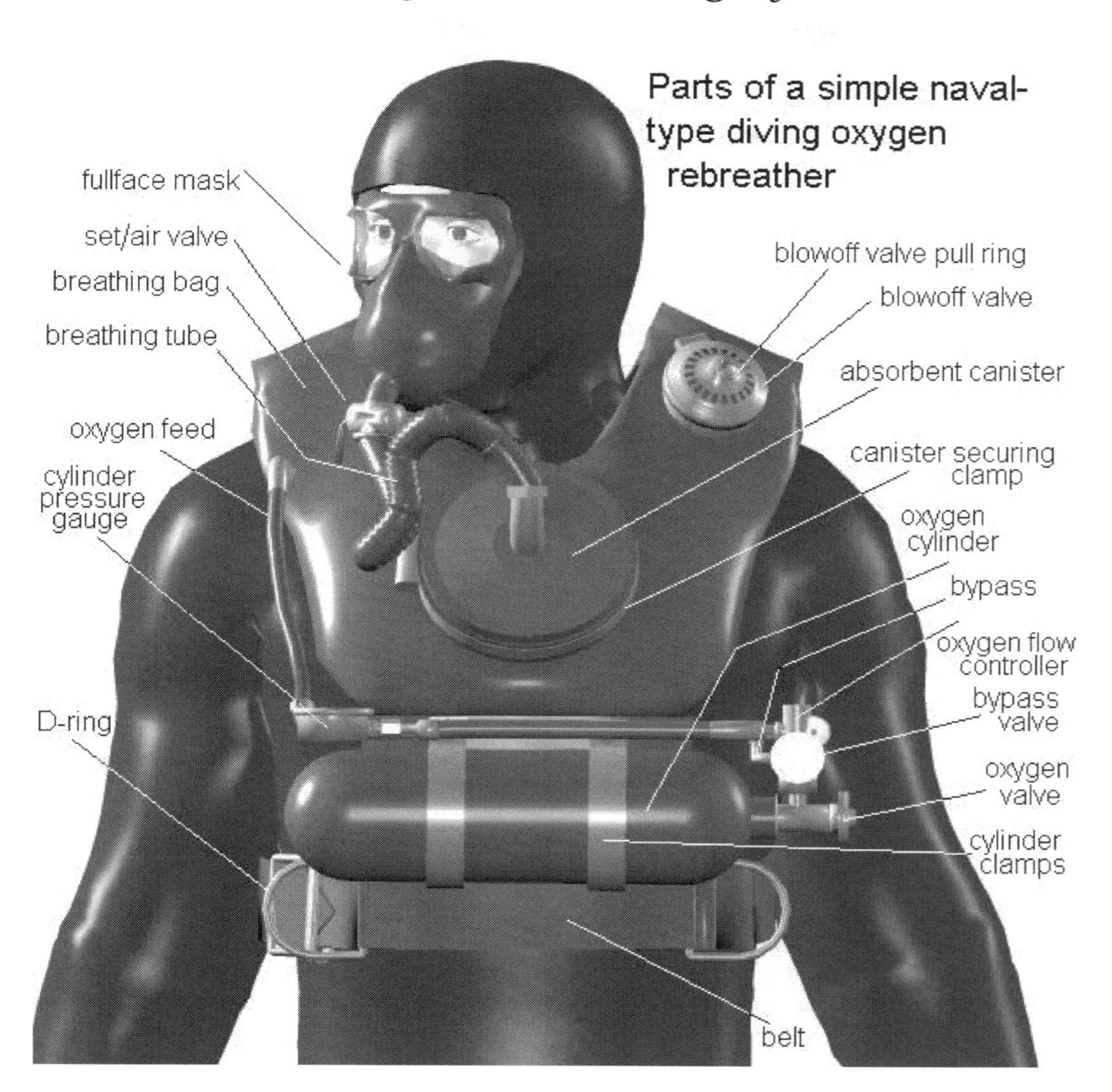

A closed circuit oxygen rebreather with a loop configuration and axial flow scrubber:

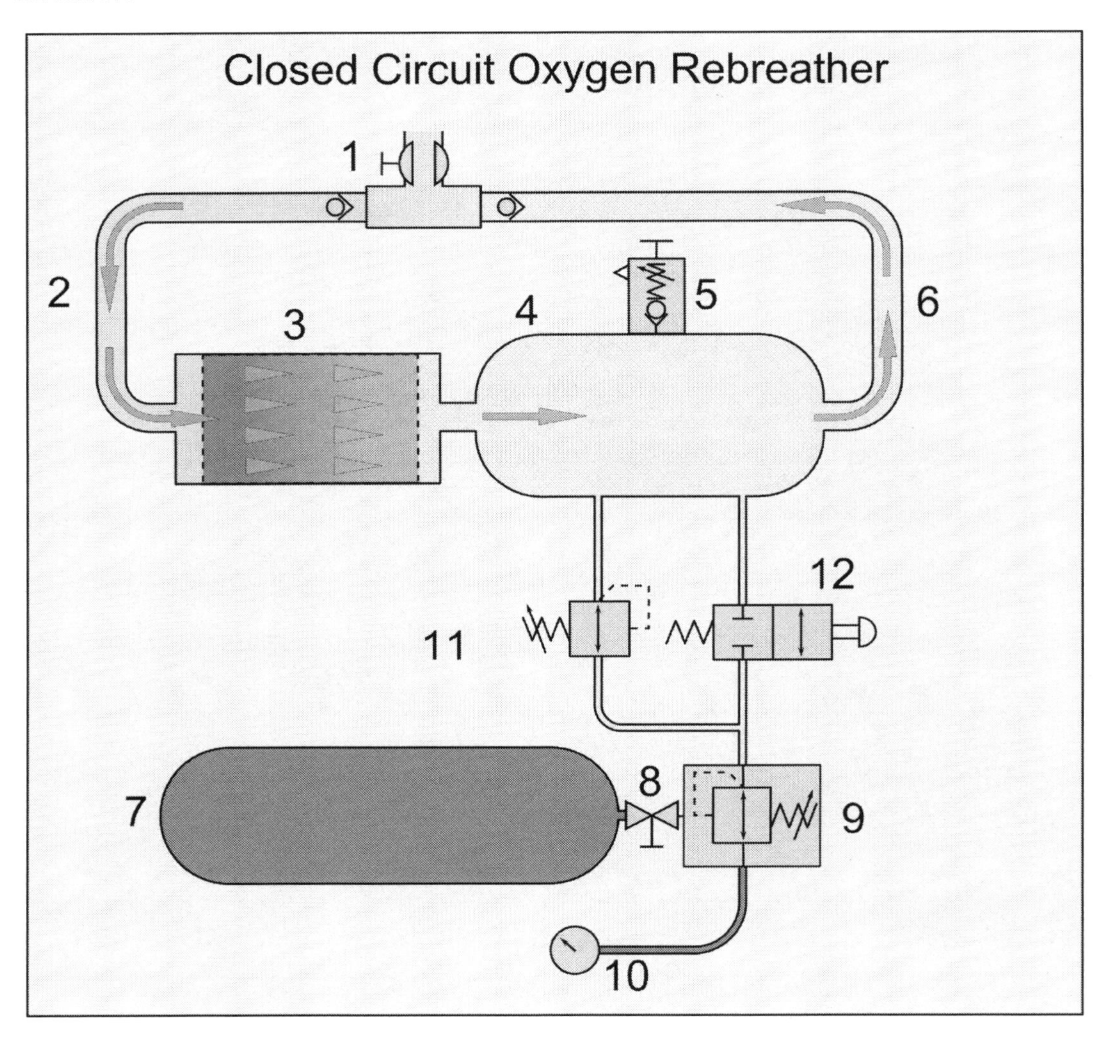

1 — Dive/surface valve with loop non return valves

2 — Exhaust hose

3 — Scrubber (axial flow)

4 — Counterlung

5 — Overpressure valve

6 — Inhalation hose

7 — Breathing gas storage cylinder

8 — Cylinder valve

9 — Regulator first stage

10 — Submersible pressure gauge

11 — Automatic make-up valve

12 — Manual bypass valve

Navy SEALs navigating underwater with an underwater compass:

Notice there are no bubbles, because of the rebreathers!

Ship attack mission

One of the missions that Navy SEALs must do is to swim underwater and place a mine on a ship. This is called the "ship attack mission" and it's part of the test to graduate from BUDS.

Two Navy SEALs partner up and swim TWO MILES underwater to the target ship.

They have to navigate underwater with nothing but a compass and a depth gauge. Once they make it to the ship, they put explosives on it, and then they have to navigate back home within a certain amount of time.

This is no easy task!

They have to place the explosive charge on the KEEL of the boat. That is the deepest and darkest part of the boat. Underwater, with the ship's engines roaring in your ear, not able to see even your hand in front of your face, you have to keep it together and accomplish the mission!

"As Navy SEALs one of our jobs is to conduct underwater attacks against enemy shipping. We practiced this technique extensively during basic training. The ship attack mission is where a pair of SEAL divers is dropped off outside an enemy harbor and then swims well over two miles —underwater—using nothing but a depth gauge and a compass to get to their target.

During the entire swim, even well below the surface, there is some light that comes through. It is comforting to know that there is open water above you. But as you approach the ship, which is tied to a pier, the light begins to fade. The steel structure of the ship blocks the moonlight, it blocks the surrounding street lamps, it blocks all ambient light.

To be successful in your mission, you have to swim under the ship and find the keel — the centerline and the deepest part of the ship. This is your objective.

But the keel is also the darkest part of the ship — where you cannot see your hand in front of your face, where the noise from the ship's machinery is deafening and where it is easy to get disoriented and fail.

Every SEAL knows that under the keel, at the darkest moment of the mission, is the time when you must be calm, composed — when all your tactical skills, your physical power and all your inner strength must be brought to bear.

If you want to change the world, you must be your very best in the darkest moment." — Admiral McRaven's Commencement speech.

VIDEO: See the rest of Admiral McRaven's speech here:

Phase 3 Land Warfare

THIRD PHASE - LAND WARFARE TRAINING

Seven weeks
More:
basic weapons,
demolitions,
land navigation,
patrolling,
rappelling,
marksmanship
and small-unit tactics

Land Warfare training lasts for seven weeks.

This is where you learn all of the combat basics on land, like:

— Clearing buildings,

— Using the different Navy SEAL weapons,

— Working with other combat units,

— And one of the best parts: DEMOLITIONS!

Clearing Buildings

Clearing a room or building is one of the many dangerous tasks Navy SEALs must perform. You don't know what or who is inside, but you gotta go in!

CQB "Close Quarters Battle" and room clearing exercise:

Watch the Navy SEALs clearing a room with a quadcopter!

This is called "Cutting the Pie":

You stand outside the open doorway, and sweep the inside of the room with your rifle, in a wide arc, "cutting the pie" and looking for any enemy combatants.

Problem: You still don't know who is standing right behind the wall in your blind spot!

In Vietnam this blind spot danger was solved by throwing a flash-bang grenade in first, and then entering the room. There are advantages to the flash-bang technique, but also, at the same time disadvantages:

1- You might kill EVERYONE in the room including women and children.

2- You ALERT everyone around you that you are there. This may be very bad if you want to keep the element of surprise and advantage!

Also part of land warfare school is DEMOLITIONS...

Blowing things up!

Demolitions are a very important part of Navy SEAL training. Explosive charges are used A LOT to breach doors and enter enemy strongholds.

Setting the explosive charges:

Kabloom! The Door is *open* now:

When you are done with Phase 3, you are done with BUD/S!

But...you are still not *done.*

BUD/S is just "BASIC" underwater demolition and SEAL training.

Now you have to go to the more advanced training, and QUALIFY as a SEAL, and get the coveted **SEAL Trident:**

SEAL Qualification Training

After phase 3 comes SEAL Qualification Training or "SQT".

This is 26 weeks long. Here you will learn the more specific SEAL tasks such as counter-terrorism and counterinsurgency.

SEAL QUALIFICATION TRAINING (SQT)

SQT is a 26-week course that will take the student from the basic elementary level of Naval Special Warfare to a more advanced degree of TACTICAL training. SQT is designed to provide students with the core tactical knowledge they will need to join a SEAL platoon

SQT:
- -- Weapons training
- -- Small unit tactics
- -- Land navigation
- -- Demolitions
- -- Cold weather training
- -- Medical skills
- -- Maritime operations

SERE training:
- -- Survival
- -- Evasion
- -- Resistance
- -- Escape

And:
- -- Static-line parachute operations
- -- Freefall parachute operations (High Altitude-Low Opening "HALO")
- -- Freefall parachute operations (High Altitude-High Opening "HAHO")

S.E.R.E. Training

S.E.R.E. training is hardcore Survival, Evasion, Resistance, and Escape training—this is what you do when you GET CAUGHT Behind Enemy Lines!

All pilots must take this training too. It's really intense: you get caught by the the enemy (played by special Navy and Air Force and Marines SERE instructors) and they torture you!—not fun!

As a matter of fact, some Navy SEALs say this is WORSE than the dreaded hell week. The psychological torture is intense as the SERE instructors act like the enemy and try to extract information from you. The main thing is to survive being captured by the enemy with Honour, and not tell him more than you need to. Good luck!

Watch the Video here:

Maritime Training

Maritime training and VBSS (Visit, Board, Search, and Seizure):

This consists of a lot of ship boarding exercises, boat maneuvering, and basically anything that has to do with ships!

Boarding ships poses many challenges, and is one of the reasons why Navy Seals are so highly trained—it is their specialty!

VBSS (Visit, Board, Search, and Seizure) Training!

VIDEO: Watch the Navy SEALs on a REAL ship boarding exercise!

Cold Weather Training

Navy SEALs have to be ready to fight in ANY weather under any conditions. That means in freezing cold water from Alaska to Siberia. The Navy SEALs have to do the jobs nobody else wants to or can do.Fighting in cold weather is also called WINTER WARFARE, and it poses many special requirements on the SEALs and their equipment.

Most of their weapons are painted white, and their uniforms are also white to blend in with the snow:

However, you don't always get to stay dry in the cold weather.

Of course Navy SEALs have to swim *regardless* of how cold it is...

Cold weather training in Alaska:

And Norway:

Finally—when you're done with all of this training, you finally graduate the SEAL school and get the SEALs trident!

Combat Operator Special Warfare Insignia.

The SEAL Trident is actually an official rating: the **Special Warfare Operator (SO) rating.**

Martial Arts

Most Navy SEALs train in MMA—Mixed Martial Arts.

Previously, Navy SEALs trained in what was called CQC: Close Quarters Combat. This programme was dropped in 2011 and now Navy SEALs train as MMA fighters in the Mixed Martial Arts.

That means a lot of Judo/Brazilian Jiu jitsu, Muy-Thai kickboxing and anything else that proves to be effective like; Boxing, Krav Maga, or even Modern-Arnis/Escrima (stick fighting).

Watch a real combat simulation with professional MMA fighters and the USMC here!

The Marine Corps have codified their Martial Arts Program, it is very much like what the Navy SEALs learn, and has proven itself as a superior fighting system:

Defense against a roundhouse punch:

Shoulder Throw (Judo/Brazilian JiuJitsu):

If you want to see the complete Marine Corps Martial Arts Program, which is very much like the Navy SEALs MMA program, check out this full PDF: **273 pages that show you the complete program**—from beginner to advanced—it's FREE:

You can get the complete MCMAP here!

The SEAL Teams

The Navy Seals follow a simple numbering system.

All of the odd numbered teams are based in Coronado California, whereas all of the even numbered teams are based on the east coast, in Virginia.

All SEAL teams have the same qualifications, so there's not much difference in the tactics that they use, however, as they are based on different coasts of the United States, the teams based in California will handle more operations in the Pacific, and the teams based in Virginia will handle more operations based in Europe or the Middle East.

YES...one team is indeed special, and it is harder to get in than all of the rest. Read on to see which one it is!

Naval Special Warfare Group ONE *Coronado California*		
Team	**Area**	**Environment**
SEAL Team 1	Western Pacific	Jungle, Desert, Urban
SEAL Team 3	Middle East	Desert, Urban
SEAL Team 5	Korea	Arctic, Desert, Urban
SEAL Team 7	Western Pacific	Jungle, Desert, Urban

Naval Special Warfare Group TWO *Little Creek, Virginia*		
Team	**Area**	**Environment**
SEAL Team 2	Northern Europe	Desert, Urban
SEAL Team 4	South+Central America	Desert, Urban
SEAL Team 8	Southern Europe	Desert, Urban
SEAL Team 10	Southern Europe	Desert, Urban

West Coast SEAL Teams:

SEAL TEAM 1

SEAL TEAM 3

SEAL TEAM 5

SEAL TEAM 7

East Coast SEAL Teams

SEAL TEAM 2

SEAL TEAM 4

SEAL TEAM 8

SEAL TEAM 10

SEAL TEAM 9

There is no Seal Team 9!

Isn't that strange?

There is much lore, and fiction, and rumours about a potential Seal Team 9, but there is no evidence that they ever existed!

That leaves us with just one other, did you notice which number was not mentioned yet?

YES! It's SEAL TEAM 6!

SEAL Team 6 is truly the elite team of the Navy SEALs.

During the Iran Hostage Crisis of 1980, the United States launched Operation Eagle Claw. It was a total failure, and eight American servicemen died.

The Navy recognized that they needed a dedicated anti-terrorist unit.

Dick Marcinko was given the task of forming a super elite team to accomplish this task. His commander's orders to him were "Dick, you will not fail!"

In 1987 SEAL Team 6 was dissolved and renamed into the Naval Special Warfare Development Group, or "DEVGRU".

DEVGRU is part of the Joint Special Operations Command or JSOC. They are also called Task Force Blue or simply "Six".

The SEALs in DEVGRU, are tasked with the most top secret missions in the world. They also are most likely to participate with the U.S. Army's Delta Force in joint operations.

SEAL Team 6 is now the number one counter-terrorism unit that specializes in hostage rescue, special reconnaissance, direct action against high-value targets, personal security, and other specialized missions.

"Counter" also means that they can strike preemptively, to PREVENT a terrorist attack.

This is the team that took out Osama bin Laden and performed the rescue of Captain Perry.

TEAM SIX was formed in 1981 when there were only 2 teams, SEAL Team 1 and 2.

Why did they skip the numbering? Where was SEAL Team 3, 4, and 5? Answer: The Legendary SEAL, Dick Marcinko, who formed SEAL Team 6, wanted to confuse the Soviets—so he skipped the numbers!

SEAL Team 6 is now the hardest team to get into—they have their own EXTRA training requirements and screening process (more tests!) Team 6 is the best of the best!

They were secret until recently—and were chosen for the most top-level, top-secret, special forces operations like the Raid on Osama Bin Laden which you can read about in the upcoming chapter.

The original SEAL Team 6 Patch:

Counter-Terrorism

What is counter-terrorism?

Under normal circumstances, we go to war and fight an enemy. Simple right?

Terrorism, however, is not normal.

With terrorists we are allowed to apply "non-conventional" tactics, and strike first, BEFORE the terrorists do.

This requires massive amounts of good intelligence—valuable information about the enemy, and his movements, and intentions.

An excellent example of counter-terrorism comes from Dick Marcinko, the founder of SEAL Team 6; the team that was actually made for counter-terrorism...

In 1982, Muammar Qaddafi was training six terrorists to assassinate president Ronald Reagan.

The six assassins were professionals from Europe; West Germany, Italy, Ireland and Israel.

They were training for the hit on a secret Libyan army base, in the middle of the desert. Qaddafi promised to pay them over 1 million dollars each. But that's not the "good part"... The good part is...they were being guarded by over thirty Libyan soldiers.—But that didn't stop the SEALs!

They sent in SEAL Team 6:

12 operators from Team 6, including Dick Marcinko, inserted in the dark of night by STOL aircraft of the 160th Special Operations Aviation Regiment. They quickly eliminated the six assassins AND the thirty Libyan soldiers guarding them.

Not only that, the entire operation was being monitored by United States Lacrosse spy satellites, and the actions of SEAL Team 6 could be seen in real time! The commanding officers watched from Washington D.C. as the SEALs fingerprinted the assassins and positively identified them. Then they were extracted by the 160th SOAR—mission complete!

And the terrorists were never heard from again.

Indeed, this COVERT MISSION was never heard of until recently, when it was declassified. How's that for counter-terrorism!?

(You can read more about this in Dick Marcinko's book "Red Cell".)

HALO

H.A.L.O. means High Altitude Low Opening.

The Navy SEALs jump out of an aircraft at very HIGH altitude, but do not open their parachutes until they are very LOW to the ground.

This is HIGHLY dangerous!

If their parachute does not work they do not have enough altitude to open their back-up parachute!

This HALO tactic is done to get behind enemy lines, and <u>not</u> be seen by enemy radar:

> *"They go in under the radar."*

Also, if you are parachuting into enemy territory, you do not want to be hanging in a parachute for a long time—that just gives the enemy a huge opportunity to shoot you!

So any time you need to go in deep and fast, and undetected; HALO is the number one tactic!

Here we go...

The JUMPMASTER monitors their position over enemy territory and tells them the EXACT moment to jump...

The team "link up" during free fall...

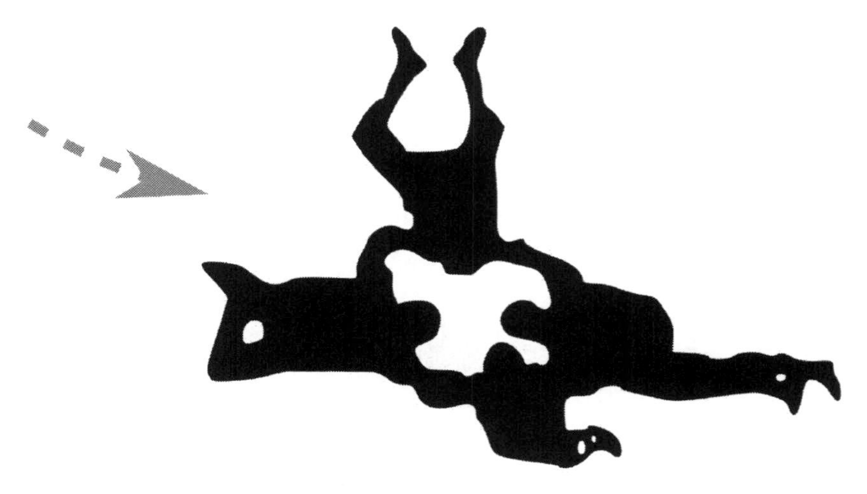

This way the team lands together on the same spot, and they can quickly gather their gear and proceed to the target!

A Hand Altimeter is used to monitor your descent. CRITICAL altitude is 3,500 feet. You MUST open your chute here!—or you don't have enough altitude to deploy your emergency parachute!

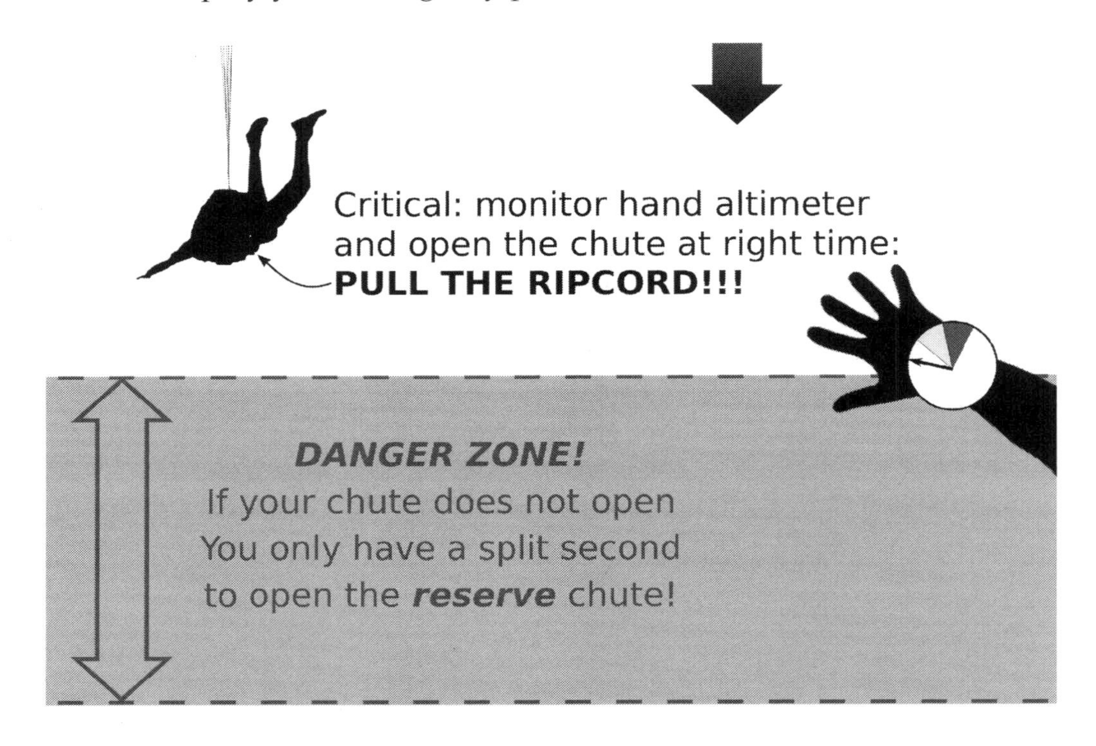

Once your 'chute is open, you fly into enemy territory. You have to land as close as possible to your LANDING ZONE where you meet up with your team and proceed to the target:

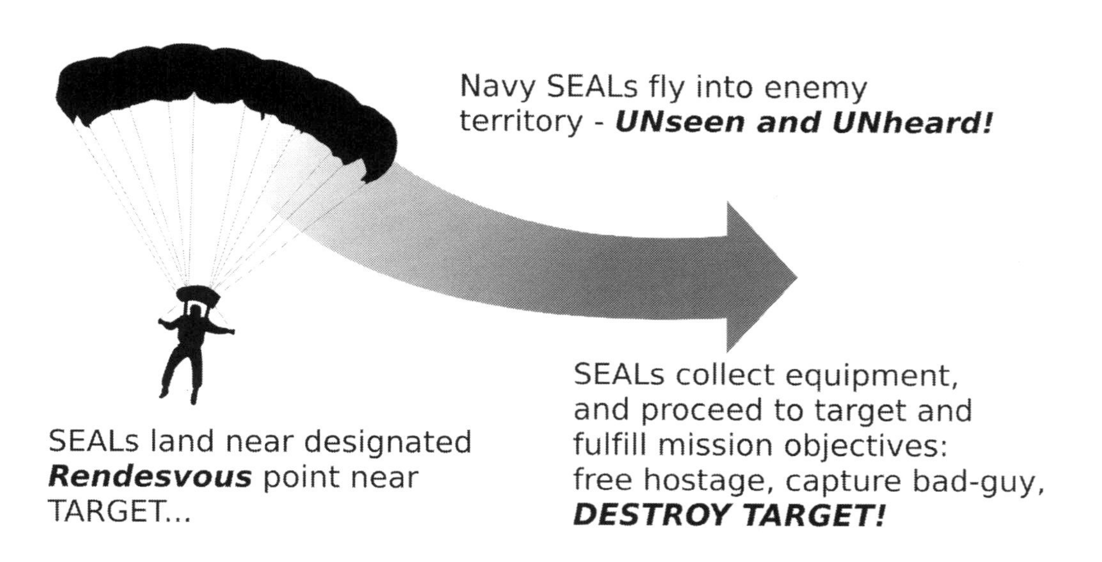

If all is done correctly, you will reach your target and have the ELEMENT of SURPRISE.

The element of surprise is super important to all special operations—it gives you the advantage over your enemy, and ensures you the upper hand in combat. The goal is to destroy the target and win, and then EXTRACT as quickly as possible.

If a mission loses its element of surprise, it is called COMPROMISED and, usually, should be aborted. However that's not always possible, as you will see in the upcoming chapter "Operation Red Wings."

You can get the full HALO infographic HERE!

SPIE and FRIES Special Patrol Insertion/Extraction

Once you're behind enemy lines—how do you get back out?!

SPIE or Special Patrol Insertion/Extraction is when the Navy SEALs "fast rope" down from a helicopter. Fast Roping is also called FRIES: Fast Rope Insertion Extraction System.

Fast roping is extremely dangerous—there is no safety system!

So if a Navy SEAL let's go of the rope, that's it—he falls to the ground!

The ropes are specially made and very thick and heavy so that the blast from the helicopter's rotors does not whip them around.

Fast roping is one of the most common insertion and extraction techniques of the Navy SEALs.

You can fast rope...

...with a dog!

...boarding a ship!

...onto a submarine!

You can also use the Fast Rope to EXTRACT from behind enemy lines. In this technique the helicopter comes to pick the team up, wherever they are, then the Navy SEALs all get on the rope at the same time and "lock in" with a carabiner:

Weapons of the Navy SEALs

All weapons used by the United States Military have to go through many tests to prove their toughness and ability to fire in combat, and the most adverse situations imaginable.

For example, when the United States was looking for a new service pistol, the Beretta M9 also passed the tests along with the Sig Sauer P226. The United States government chose the Beretta M9 as the standard service pistol for all armed forces, but not because it is better than the Sig, but because it is CHEAPER.

The Navy SEALs, however, make their OWN choices, and chose back then, and now, the Sig Sauer P226 over the Beretta.

The Navy SEALs demand a lot from their weapons. They don't use the standard issue weapons of the Army or Navy. Instead, they prefer a lot of exotic European weapons like Heckler and Koch and Belgian FN SCAR rifles, or the Carl Gustav recoilless rifle from Sweden. The right tool for the right job!

Sig Sauer P226

The Sig Sauer P226 is one of the most reliable and accurate handguns ever built.

In order to be chosen for the Navy SEALs the P226 had to pass rigorous tests in the laboratory and in real combat.

For example, the pistol is thrown in the mud and then fired with all of the dirt in the barrel and receiver—they really try to break the gun!

And during these tests it is also submerged underwater and fired.

They also cycle thousands of rounds as fast as possible with firing machines that just keep pulling the trigger, round after round, just trying to make the gun break!

Heckler & Koch USP

The H&K USP is another favorite of the Navy Seals.

Notice it has a rail underneath the barrel where you can attach anything from laser sights to flashlights and infra-red lasers.

USP means "Universal Self-loading Pistol" and the Navy Seals use the 45 calibre version, the "HK45".
In 2011 the HK45 Compact won the gruelling tests to be the Navy's new "SOCOM" (Special Operations Command) pistol and replace the MK 23 pistol.

The HK45C is not only used by Navy SEALs but other Naval Special Warfare personnel.

They renamed it to MK 24 Mod 0 Combat Assault Pistol.

Standard accessories are:

- AAC suppressor
- Waterproof IR laser

Heckler & Koch MP5

The standard H&K MP5 with a 40 round magazine:

The H&K MP5 is one of the most popular submachine guns in the world.

They're very tough, accurate, and waterproof.

You see Navy SEALs with these a lot in pictures when they're coming out of the water.

You can put almost anything on this submachine gun: lasers, high powered scopes, red dot sights, flashlights, large capacity magazines, you name it!

It shoots a 9mm bullet at 800 rounds per minute.

That means you pull the trigger once and it can shoot 800 rounds—IF you could load that many in the magazine.

The standard MP5 magazine only holds 40 rounds (bullets).

The Beta C Mag Drum magazine however holds 100 rounds. That means you would need 8 of these "drum" magazines just to shoot for 1 minute at a constant rate!

H&K MP5 with a forearm pistol grip and folding stock.

"MP" means "maschinenpistole" in German, or "machine pistol". Unlike a machine-gun which fires rifle bullets, a machine-pistol fires pistol bullets (much smaller!) like the 9mm Parabellum:

9mm Parabellum Rounds and Bullet

M4A1

Finally an American gun!

The M4A1: Calibre 5.56 x 49 mm NATO, is very versatile and is based on the M-16 Assault Rifle, the standard rifle of the US armed forces.

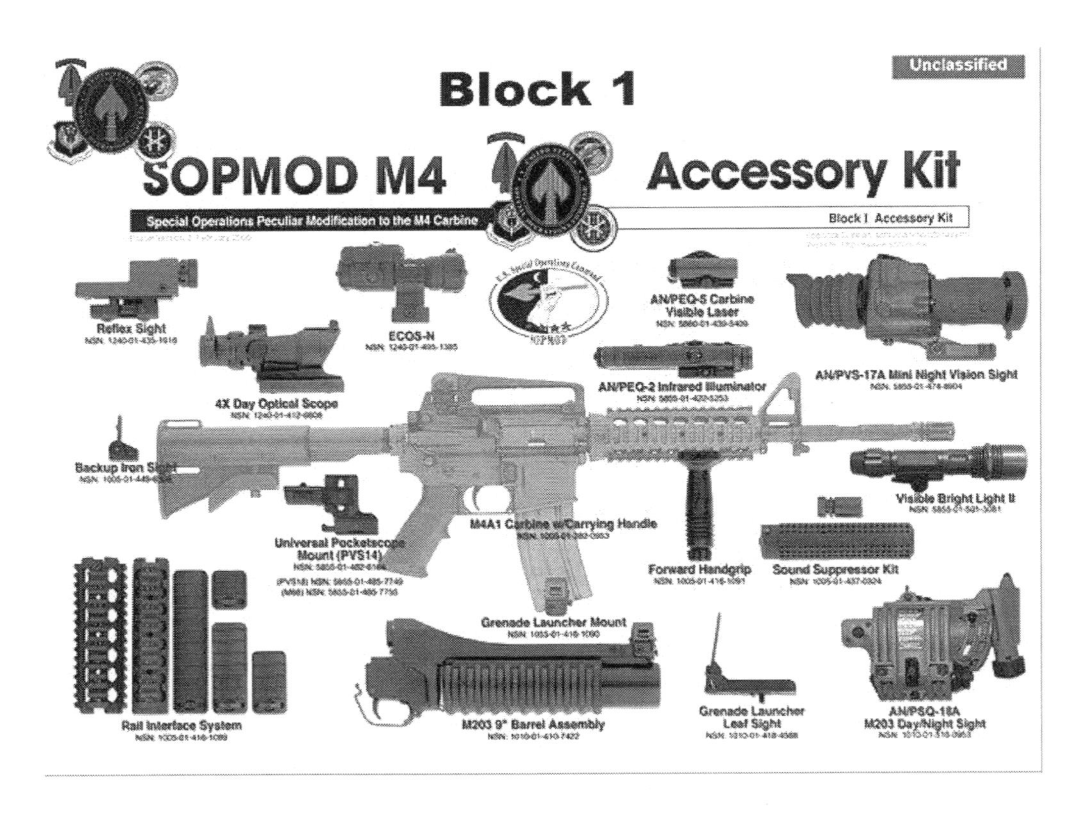

You can mix and match the M4A1 almost anyway you want, you can even put a GRENADE LAUNCHER on it:

The inner workings of a semi-automatic M16 rifle; showing the hammer hitting the firing pin inside the bolt. Also shown is the gas tube which siphons some of the hot gases from the barrel as the bullet fires and uses them to unlock the bolt, move it backwards, eject the spent casing, and returning forward, to pull a new round from the magazine and chamber it in the barrel:

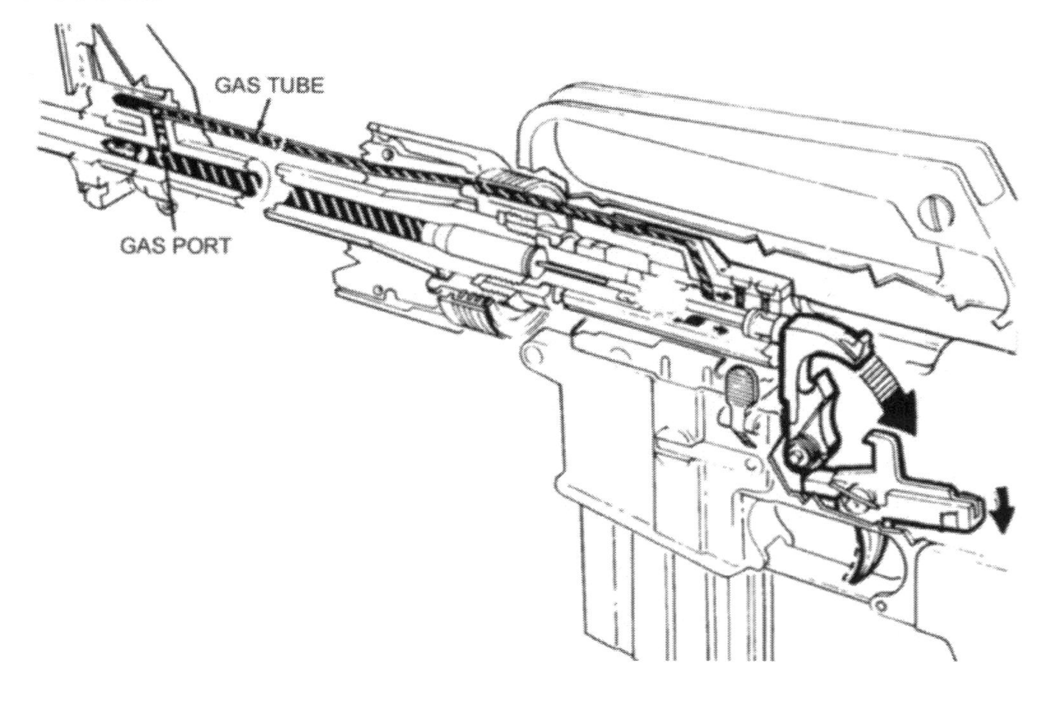

Note: The M4A1 is frequently confused with the M16 and the Colt AR-15. However, the M4A1 is a newer version of the M16.

The M16 was the original version of this rifle, which replaced the M-14 as the standard-issued rifle of the United States armed forces in 1968. The colt AR-15 is the civilian version of the M-16 which is sold in gun stores worldwide.

HK 416

The HK416 also shoots the 5.56 x 49mm calibre round, just like the M4A1.

The HK has long rails on top of, and below the barrel for the various accessories like pistol grips, laser sights, and grenade launchers:

You may be wondering why it looks so similar to the M4A1, that's because its receiver is *almost* exactly the same as the M4A1's.

The receiver is the central core of the gun to which everything else attaches:

- The stock
- The pistol grip
- The trigger group
- The magazine
- The barrel
- The top rail or sight mount

The receiver also houses the most important part of the gun: the bolt. The bolt takes the bullet out of the magazine and puts it into the barrel and, along with the hammer and firing pin, fires it.

The upper and lower receiver of the Colt AR-15:

The HK416 was built to be interchangeable with many M4A1 parts, For example, both the M4A1 end hk416 can use the same magazines.

Claim to Fame:

The HK416 was used by the Navy SEALs to kill Osama bin Laden!

(see the upcoming chapter "The Raid on Osama Bin Laden".)

Carl Gustaf 84mm Recoilless Rifle

The Carl Gustav recoilless rifle is definitely one of the Navy SEALs favorite weapons. You always hear them speaking fondly of it—it's the mother of all boomsticks!

It shoots an 84 mm projectile out of a rifled barrel. The rifled barrel spins the projectile and stabilizes it. This makes it much more accurate and increases its effective range.

A recoilless rifle works on the principle of inertia:

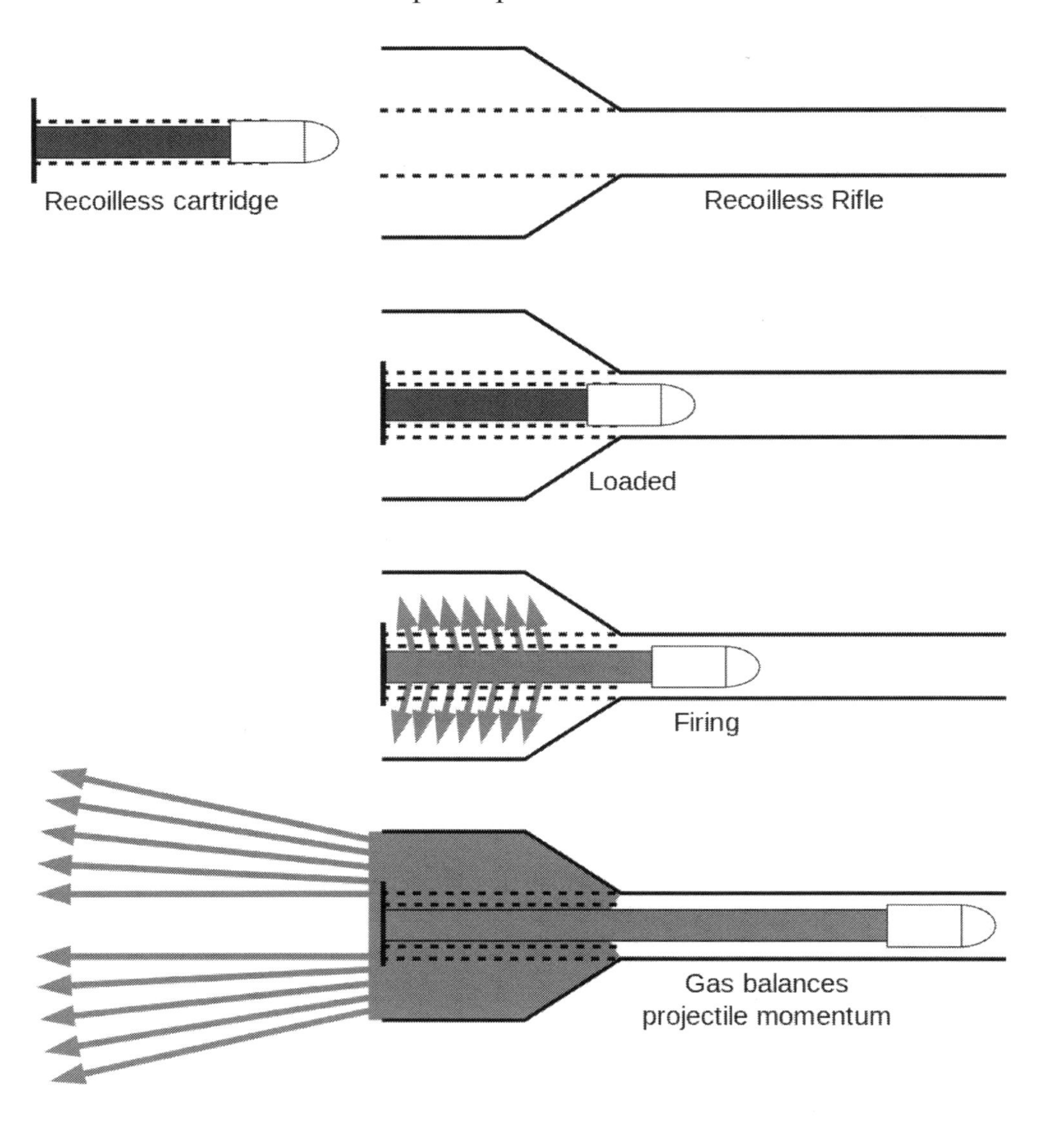

Unlike a rocket launcher, that launches a rocket with a constant burn from the rocket motor, recoilless rifles work more like a gun that shoots a bullet or projectile.

The Carl Gustaf can hit moving targets as far as 400 meters away, and stationary targets at 500 meters!

Just like the other rifles and submachine guns of the Navy Seals, you can put a telescopic sight, a laser rangefinder, or even a night-vision sight on this recoilless rifle.

If you load it with the FFV751 tandem-warhead HEAT round, the Carl Gustaf can penetrate up to 500mm of armor. That means you could take out a light tank or armored vehicle with the Carl Gustaf!

HEAT stands for High Explosive Anti Tank and they were developed in World War II just to penetrate armored vehicles.

<u>**AT4 Recoilless Rifle**</u>

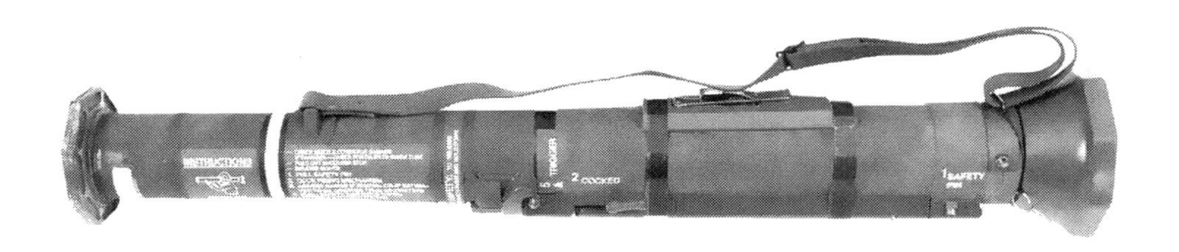

Because they work on the principle of INERTIA, all recoilless rifles have a HUGE BACKBLAST.

If anyone is standing behind an AT4 or Carl Gustaf when they fire it—it would kill them!

The AT-4 is a "throw-away" rocket launcher. It is very light but very powerful at the same time. Once it is used, you throw away the tube launcher.

The AT4 is like a cheaper, lighter version of the Carl Gustav recoilless rifle, and it also shoots an 84mm projectile.

However the AT4 has the advantage that it is much lighter and easier to carry around. That makes a BIG difference when you have a long march to your target.

However, it doesn't pack such a punch as the Carl Gustav, but it is effective enough!

Like the Carl Gustaf the AT4 is also a recoilless rifle, but it does not have rifling, instead it has a smooth bore. This means its projectiles must have fins and be "fin stabilized".

An AT4 being used in a real firefight in Iraq!

The Navy SEALs Everlasting Anthem:

Eternal Father, faithful friend,

Be swift to answer those we send,

In brotherhood and urgent trust,

On hidden missions dangerous,

O hear us when we cry to Thee,

For SEALs in air, on land, and sea.

Night vision

Night vision is very important. It gives the Navy SEALs a huge advantage in most areas of the world. Night vision is also very expensive, and most of the terrorists and enemy combatants don't have it. When there is a big difference in technologies and skills between combatants, it is called "ASYMMETRIC WARFARE".

Night vision goggles use an IMAGE INTENSIFIER to amplify the light. Even in darkness there is a little light, especially on a moonlit night.

Photons (light) go in, and MORE come out = night vision!

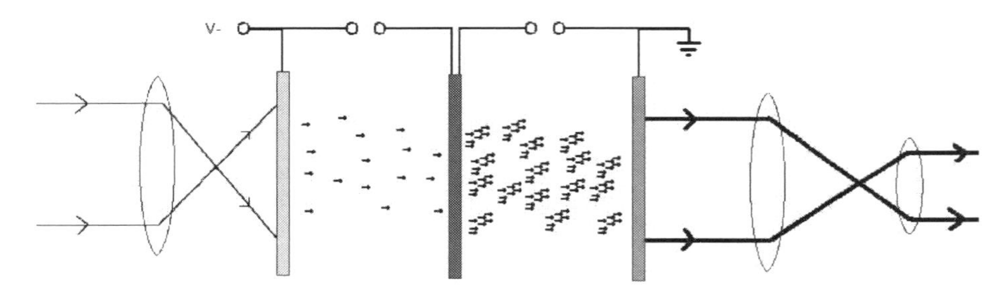

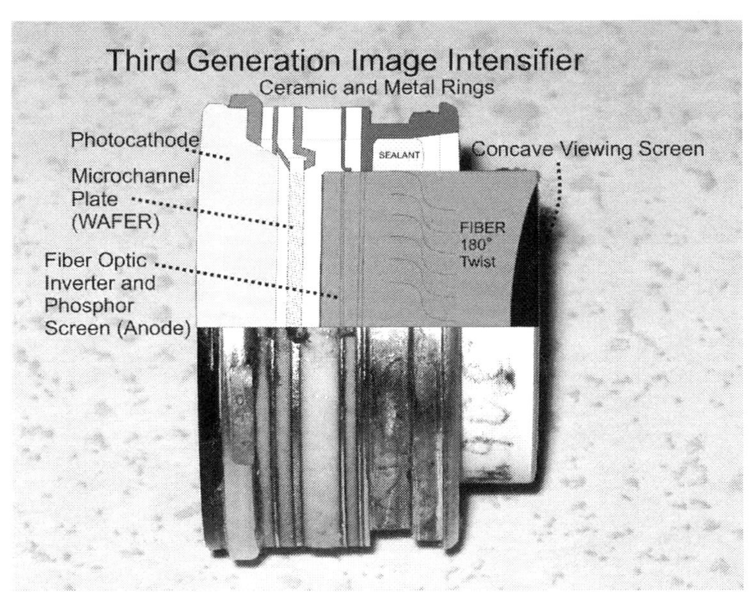

The image intensifier does this ELECTRONICALLY. Another word for it is "photo-multiplier."

For every PHOTON entering the tube, the intensifier will emit more than came in. This way you can take the little bit of light available at night, MULTIPLY it, and see in the dark.

There is only one small disadvantage to night vision... it's ALL GREEN!

Question: How do you aim your rifle when you are wearing night vision goggles?

Answer: With the INFRA-RED LASER mounted on your rifle!

When you are wearing night vision goggles, you cannot use the normal sight on your rifle.

Instead, you use the infra-red laser and point it at your target. Wherever the laser light dot appears, your bullet will hit!

Infra-red light is invisible to the naked eye, but your night vision goggles can see it.

But beware: sometimes the enemy has night vision goggles too, and can see your laser, and YOU!

The newest generation of PANORAMA night vision goggles:

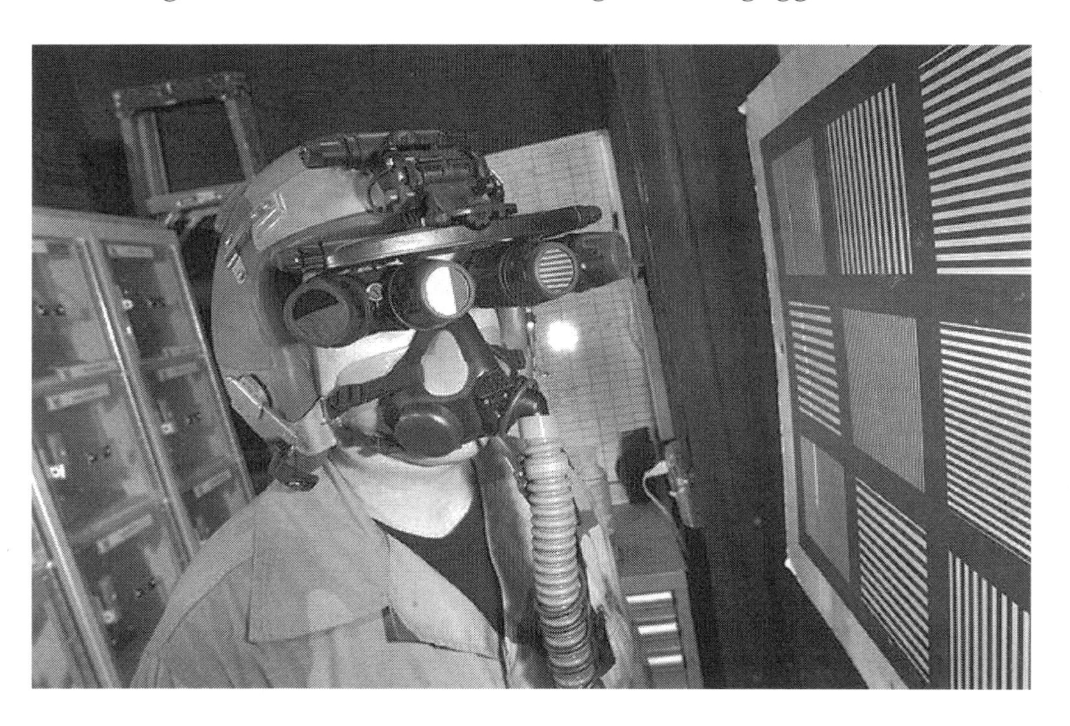

The Navy is now working on an underwater night vision device for underwater combat. Can you imagine fighting underwater? Well the Navy Seals can, and do!

How much does a Navy SEAL make?

Navy SEALs are paid based on their RANK.

Just like any other member of the Navy, their pay is the same no matter what they do...it all depends on their rank AND if they are in a war zone or not.

So it is hard to calculate a SEAL's pay, unless you know if they are in an active war zone or not.

Here are the base pay grades for officers and enlisted personnel of the US Navy as of 2016.

Remember: you get more when you go to war.

"E"—Enlisted Ranks:

Pay Grade	**Years of Service**				
	Less than 2	**Over 2**	**Over 3**	**Over 4**	**Over 6**
E-7	2816	3074	3191	3347	3469
E-6	2436	2680	2798	2913	3033
E-5	2232	2381	2496	2614	2798
E-4	2046	2151	2267	2382	2483
E-3	1847	1963	2082	2082	2082
E-2	1756	1756	1756	1756	1756
E-1	1567	1567	1567	1567	1567

"O"—Officer Ranks:

Pay Grade See Note 1&2	Years of Service				
	Under 2	Over 2	Over 3	Over 4	Over 6
O-8	9946	10272	10488	10549	10819
O-7	8264	8649	8826	8967	9223
O-6	6267	6885	7337	7337	7365
O-5	5224	5886	6293	6370	6624
O-4	4508	5218	5567	5644	5967
O-3	3963	4493	4850	5287	5540
O-2	3425	3900	4492	4644	4739
O-1	2972	3094	3740	3740	3740

The Difference Between the Others

What do Navy SEALs do that the others don't?

How about deployment by submarines!?

The main difference between the Navy SEALs and the others is their affinity for water—they are a MARITIME Force, entering and leaving the battle zone by water. For example, Navy SEALs also specialize in MINI-SUBMARINES!

Of course they have a special name too: SEAL DELIVERY VEHICLE, or SDV.

Below we see SEAL Delivery Vehicle Team Two (SDVT-2) launching one of the team's SEAL Delivery Vehicles (SDV) from the back of the USS Philadelphia, SSN 690. The SDVs are used to carry Navy SEALs from the still submerged submarine to enemy targets while staying underwater and undetected.

They then deliver the payload, a TORPEDO to destroy the enemy ship!

After the mission, they maneuver the SDV back into the "ASDS":

The submarines that deploy them must be modified too. This is called the ADVANCED SEAL DELIVERY SYSTEM, or ASDS. That hump on the back of this submarine is carrying a Seal Delivery Vehicle inside:

Below we see the ASDS attached to the back of the USS Greeneville during sea testing off the coast of Pearl Harbor Hawaii:

What if there is no SEAL Delivery Vehicle at hand?

Have no fear! We can shoot the Navy SEALs out of the torpedo tubes, without any vehicle!

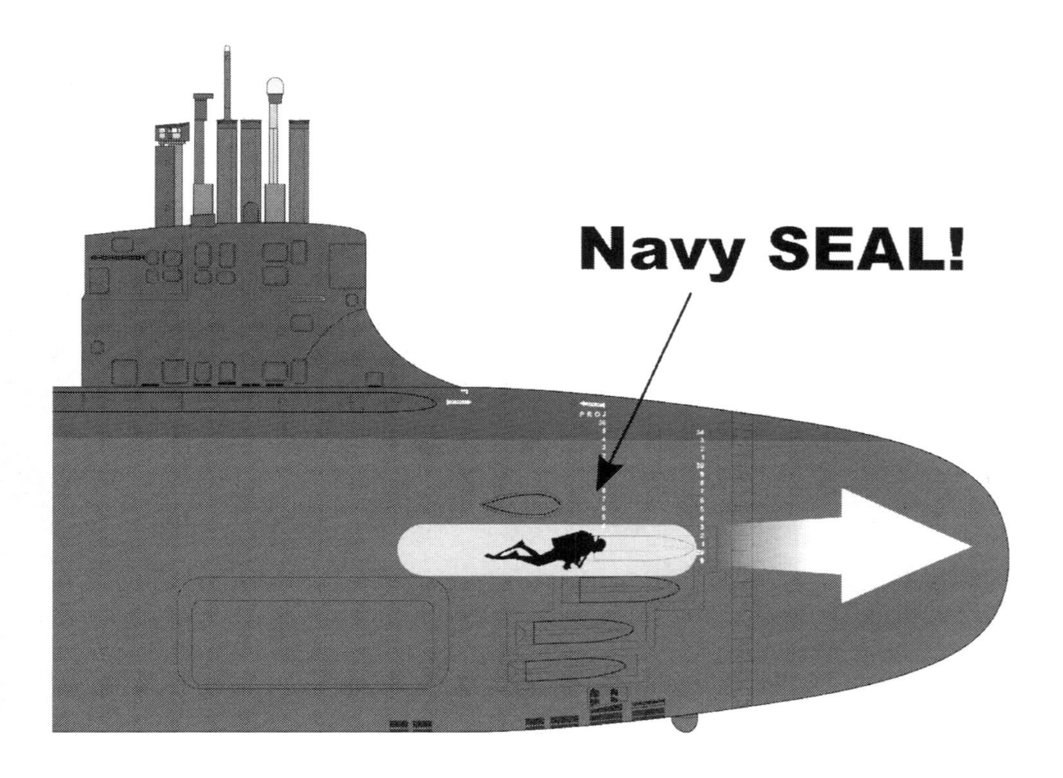

Scan here for the AMAZING video!

SWCC - Special Boat Teams

The "Special Warfare Combatant-craft Crewmen" is a separate Special Operations team which specializes in taking Navy SEALs to where they need to go—near the water, and undetected. This is called "Insertion" or "Extraction" depending if they are coming or going.

Special Boat Team 12's patch:

SWCC combat crewmen and Navy SEALs go through very similar, but separate training at the Naval Amphibious Base in Coronado.

As a matter of fact, they go through the SAME training as a SEAL right until Hell Week. Here they split off from the "normal" Navy SEAL training pipeline and go off to do more specific training that has to do with boats, VERY FAST and armed boats!

"Surgical strikes" are one of the typical tasks of the Navy SEALs and SWCC; get in and get out fast! Hit an exact target with super precision, and take it out, then disappear!

The SWCC crewmen are also airborne, like the Navy SEALs, and parachute with their boats.

Watch the SWCC throw their "little" boats out of a C-17 Globemaster and then deploy them!

Watch the Video Here:

They can also deploy by helicopter:

Anytime the Navy SEALs need a "Hot Extract"—the SWCC is ready to go in and lay down covering fire!

A Navy SEAL boatman blasts out over 6,000 rounds per minute with the M134 Minigun:

The boats of the SWCC are bristling with firepower!

No matter what angle you choose, they have a machine gun to cover you!

See a REAL "HOT EXTRACT" here!

Get Extracted by the Navy SEALs and the SWCC!

Animals

Another thing Navy SEALs do that no one else does is work with Sea Lions and Dolphins!

Yes, other teams use animals like dogs (the Navy SEALs also have a combat dog team,) but the Navy also uses MARINE ANIMALS:

- Dolphins are used to protect boats and detect enemy divers.
- Sea Lions are used to detect underwater mines and enemy divers!

Sea Lions are used to locate mines and bombs underwater. Once a Sea Lion does find one, he will then put a radio locator on it, so the Navy can find it and destroy it:

Underwater there is no more capable or effective animal than a sea lion. They can even out swim great white sharks!

[CLASSIFIED!]

The existence of the following programs can neither be confirmed nor denied!

If you can train an animal to find a mine, you can also train one to...

- PLANT a mine
- Attach bombs to ships…
- Attack enemy divers who are trying to bomb YOUR ship…
- Plant listening devices…

However... Marine animals are VERY expensive to take care of.

The US Navy is exploring the possibility of replacing all of their marine animals with underwater robots and drones.

Although the underwater robots cannot match the accuracy and sensitivity of a sea lion's nose underwater— they are much cheaper and easier to maintain.

For example, if you need to find a mine near a ship, you just transport your underwater robot to the area, and deploy it. Not so easy with animals! The transport of a sea lion or dolphin is very difficult, and the animals can even die on the way to the combat theatre.

You can see more of the Navy's NMMP here:

Navy SEAL Dogs!

Navy SEALs dogs are one of the SEAL Teams' top "secret" weapons! Their COMBAT DOGS go wherever the Navy SEALs go—even if they jump out of a plane at high altitude!

Dogs are used just about on every mission, for example, they were used to get the #1 terrorist in the world Osama Bin Laden, and just recently they were used to get Abu Bakr al-Baghdadi; the last terrorist leader of ISIS!

Conan the special forces Hero Dog who got the ISIS terrorist!

The Navy SEAL teams prefer the Belgian Malinois dog.

The Malinois looks a lot like a German Shepherd—but there are some important differences:

For one, they are smaller and lighter, which makes it easier for the SEALs to carry them, and parachute with them.

But, despite being lighter than a German Shepherd, they are just as capable and ferocious!

See a real Navy SEAL Combat-Dog do a REAL Takedown here:

When the dogs parachute with the SEALs, they usually wear eye-protection goggles made JUST for dogs!

One of the main tasks of Navy SEAL dogs is to "CLEAR BUILDINGS".

Clearing buildings of terrorists is where most of the firefights are!

The following photo is of a REAL special forces dog clearing a building in Afghanistan—not practicing here!—nobody knows what is beyond the door...

Question:

Do Combat Dogs have titanium teeth?

Answer:

NO.

Titanium teeth are only used when the dog has damaged his teeth, and needs a replacement.

They are "false" teeth and are NOT stronger than their real teeth. However, they are better than nothing!

Historic Battles

The Navy SEALs have been in *every* battle since World War 2!

World War 2

It all started with the Naval Combat Demolition Units—NCDUs.

Lieutenant Commander Draper Kauffman started the Naval Combat Demolition Unit (NCDU) training school at Ft. Pierce Florida in June of 1943.

He got the toughest Navy divers from the Bomb and Mine Disposal School, and the Civil Engineering Corps, and the Naval Construction Corps (also known as the "Seabees") School at Camp Peary Virginia.

This is where LCDR Kauffman made HELL WEEK part of Navy SEAL training! By the end of the training at Ft. Pierce only 65-75% made it through to the end. Just like today in BUD/S.

Each NCDU had one boat crew: one officer and five enlisted sailors.

After several months of hardcore Navy SEAL training the first NCDU class graduated in September 1943. They specialized in clearing the beaches with explosives, and demolition of submerged beach obstacles and barriers. They knew they were going to have a tough time—the German forces had barricaded the beaches on the sand and UNDER water!

Seven NCDUs were sent to the Pacific fleets, and three units went to the Mediterranean fleet, and one NCDU went to England.

In April 1944 thirty-four NCDUs collected in England as a jump-off point for OPERATION OVERLORD, the invasion of Nazi ruled Europe at Normandy!

D-Day

It all went down on "D-Day"—the first day of the invasion.

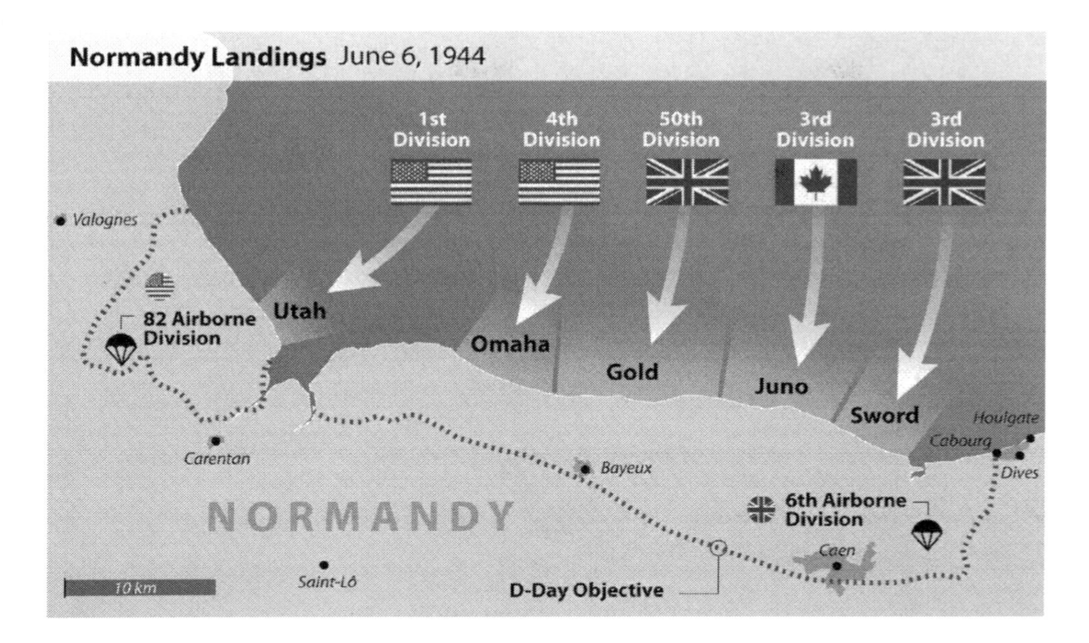

For the amphibious landing at Normandy, each six-man NCDU was upgraded to a nine-man unit with three additional U.S. Navy seamen to help in clearing the beaches and blowing things up!

The new nine-man NCDUs were then attached to U.S. Army combat engineers to form 13-man "gap assault teams." They were called gap assault teams because you have to make a GAP in the enemy lines to get through and destroy them. This was the first phase of the beach assault. Then the rest of the forces could land and drive inland towards Germany and France.

175 members in all were the first invading forces to arrive on the beaches of Normandy.

Approaching under heavy German fire, the demolitionists used explosives to clear the way for the massive invasion of some 5,000 vessels, and more than 150,000 Allied soldiers and sailors.

During the invasion on June 6, 1944 thirty-seven NCDU men were killed, and seventy-one were wounded. That's a casualty rate of 52%!

After the war the NCDUs at Omaha Beach were awarded the Presidential Unit Citation; one of only three awarded at Normandy. And the NCDUs at Utah Beach received the only Navy Unit Commendation awarded at all.

> *The Navy SEALs suffered a 52 percent casualty rate!*
>
> *It was definitely the bloodiest day in the history of the Navy SEALs.*

UDT engagements in WWII:

Operation Overlord

Operation Torch

Battle of Kwajalein

Battle of Roi Namur

Battle of Saipan

Battle of Tinian

Battle of Guam

Battle of Peleliu

Battle of Iwo Jima

Battle of Okinawa

Borneo Campaign

Battle of Leyte

Invasion of Lingayen Gulf

Okinawa

Some of the most intense, legendary fighting ever, happened on the island of Okinawa in Japan in World War 2.

The Japanese forces had built a long network of tunnels and caves in the mountains of the island. They housed their provisions and powerful guns there. They were "dug in" and nothing was going to get them out...but a concerted effort of ALL the allied forces!

War flag of the Imperial Japanese Army (1870–1945):

Just one of the tunnel systems under an Okinawan mountain:

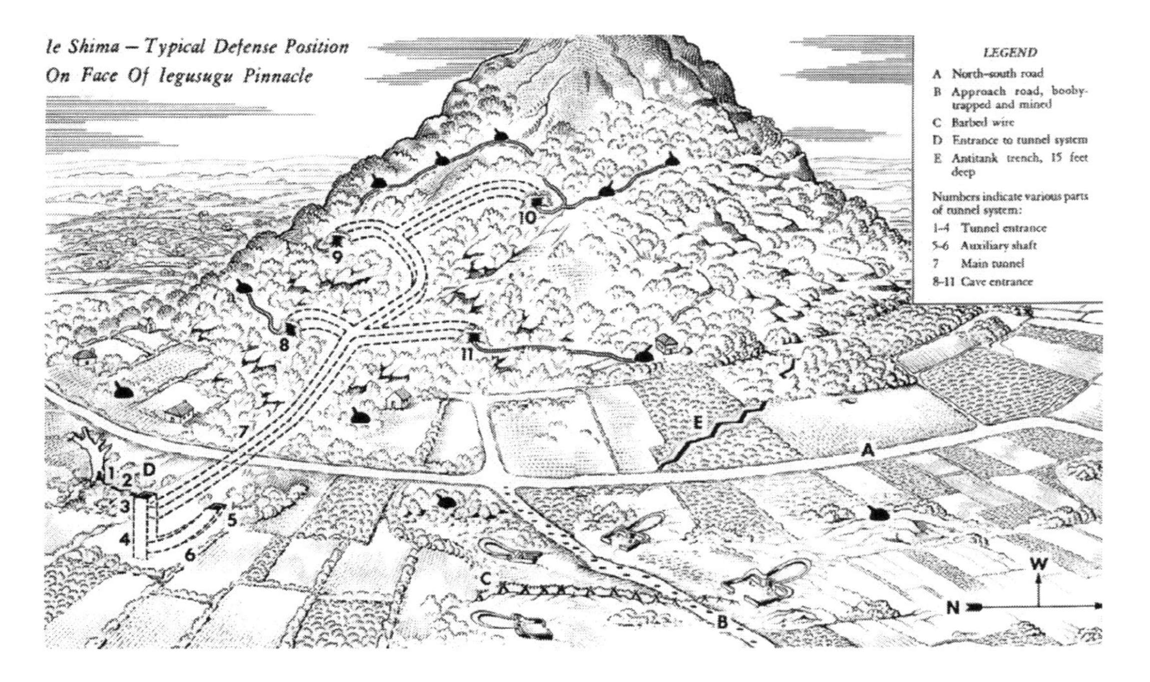

A Japanese 150mm howitzer in the tunnels of Okinawa:

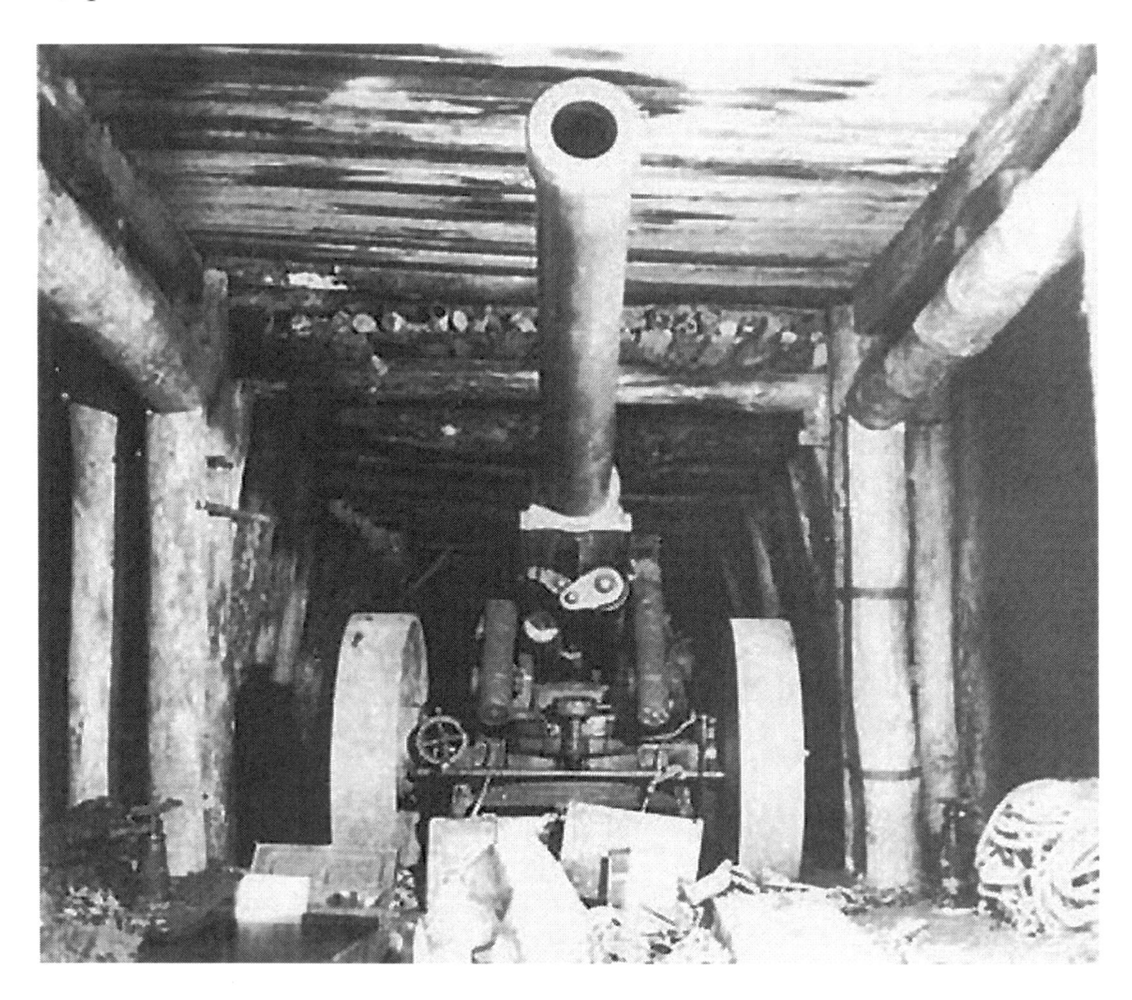

The Battle of Okinawa, codenamed Operation Iceberg, was a HUGE battle involving battleships, aircraft, tanks, and all of the fighting units of the Japanese Imperial Army, versus the United States Marines and Navy and Army forces.

And of course the Navy SEALs were there! However...

During World War 2, they weren't called Navy SEALs yet, they were "Underwater Demolition Teams", or UDT—FROGMEN!

They even have a frog chewing a stick of dynamite as their insignia:

The United States Marines had previously lost 3,000 Marines (yes—three THOUSAND!) in the Battle of Tarawa in November 1943, so they turned to the Navy Special Operation forces to infiltrate, navigate and gather intelligence of the islands of the South Pacific BEFORE the invasion of Okinawa.

It was the crucial last step in the allies Island hopping campaign towards mainland Japan.

By far this was the largest UDT operation of WWII involving teams 7, 11, 12, 13, 14, 16, 17, and 18, that's 1,000 men!

The ocean around Okinawa added an extra element of danger for the divers —it's really cold, and could cause hypothermia and severe cramps, and death. In World War 2 they did not have good "wetsuits" and the UDT Frogmen were risking their lives in all operations around Okinawa. Operations included both reconnaissance, and demolition at the landing beaches, and feints to create the illusion of landings in other locations.

Like D-Day in Normandy, the Frogmen of the U.S. Navy were tasked with clearing the beaches for the invasion: the Japanese Imperial Army fortified the beaches against invasions with pointed poles and metal barricades set into the coral reefs.

UDT teams 11 and 16 were sent in to blast them apart. The explosive charges took out all of UDT 11's targets and half of UDT 16's. However, UDT 16 was struck with bad luck, and one of their men died during the operation. UDT 11 went back the next day and finished the job, after which they remained to guide invasion craft to the beach.

Marines landing on the Okinawa beaches, cleared and made safe by the UDT Frogmen:

Marines demolishing a cave on Okinawa:

Okinawa was the bloodiest battle of the Pacific War.

There were 240,931 casualties including 149,193 Okinawan civilians, 77,166 Imperial Japanese soldiers, 14,009 American soldiers.

The Americans suffered over 82,000 casualties.

At the end of the war, 34 UDT teams had been created with teams 1–21 having actually been sent to war. Over half of the men in the teams came from the Seabees:

The Seabees are the United States Naval Construction Battalions, from the U.S. Naval Construction Force (NCF).

From the words **C**onstruction **B**attalion we get "C B" = Seabee!

Even back then, these "proto" Navy SEALs were special forces, and they were kept secret. The U.S. Navy did not publicize the existence of the UDTs until after the war, and when they did, they gave credit where credit is due; to Lt. Commander Kauffman and the Seabees.

The Vietnam War

Finally, the Navy SEALs are now officially called ... Navy SEALs, and Navy SEAL teams, because of their ability to operate in all environments: sea, air, and land.

In Vietnam the first objective was training with the indigenous South Vietnamese forces.

There were only two SEAL teams back then:

SEAL Team 1, and SEAL Team 2:

They formed 12 men SEAL platoons and rotated in and out of action in South Vietnam, performing commando missions, and honing their battle skills, and shaping up their reputation as elite Special Forces

Back then PBR Boats (Patrol Boat Riverine) were their standard method of insertion and extraction along the Mekong river delta.

A Bell UH-1E "Huey" flies over a PBR boat during a riverine patrol in Vietnam in 1967:

They engaged in guerilla warfare in the jungles of Viet Nam!

Navy SEALs deployed from boats, and helicopters, and carried out short direct action missions like ambushes, hit and run raids, personnel recovery, and intelligence and reconnaissance missions.

The Vietcong hated the Navy SEALs and called them "The men with green faces" because of the green and black camouflage paint that they wore on their face.

They fought for over six years in Vietnam and inflicted heavy losses on the enemy: 600 confirmed kills and 300 most certainly killed.

Although most "conventional" forces pulled out of Vietnam, the SEALs stayed there until 1973.

The Mark II Patrol Boat—the real workhorse of the U.S. Navy in the Vietnam war:

The Mekong river in Vietnam:

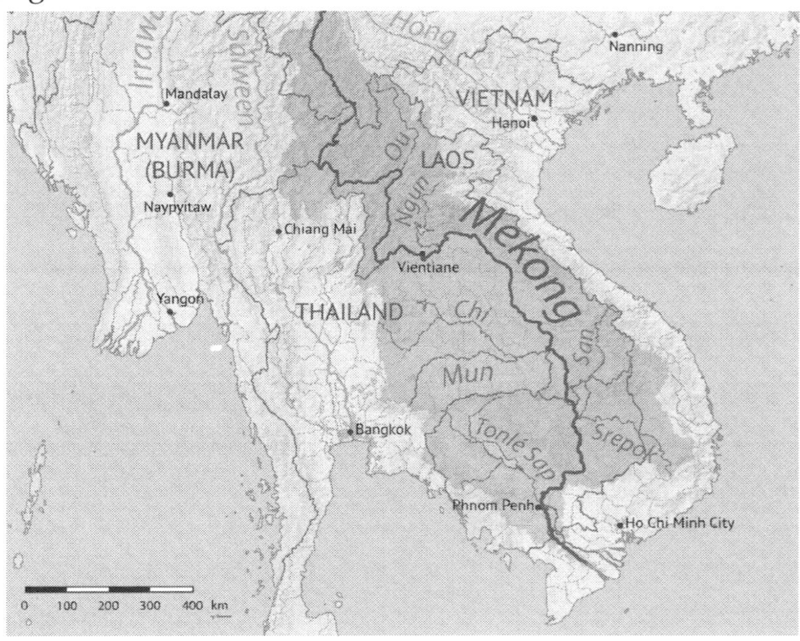

Grenada: Operation Urgent Fury

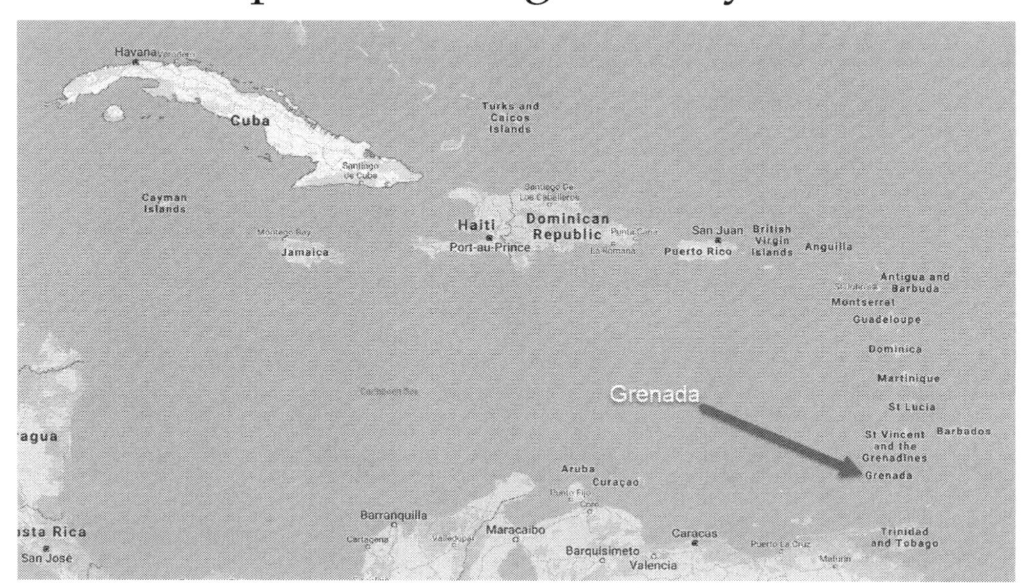

In 1983 the Cold War was still raging.

Tension between communist Cuba and the United States was constantly being tested by Fidel Castro and his Soviet overlords.

Castro decided to send his own special forces to help his agent Hudson Austin capture a small island nation called Grenada.

They captured Grenada's prime minister Maurice Bishop...and killed him! Then they set up their own government and proceeded to take over the island, and the Universities of the island...which had over 600 American students.

This could have easily blown-up into a full World War!

President Reagan launched operation Urgent Fury to kick the communists out, and protect the American students on the island, and also to free the mayor of Grenada, who had been taken hostage by the "Communist rebels" which were mostly Cuban special forces in disguise.

This mission was not perfect.

Four Navy SEALs were lost in the early morning hours as they deployed their rafts in very bad weather and surf on the Grenada beaches.

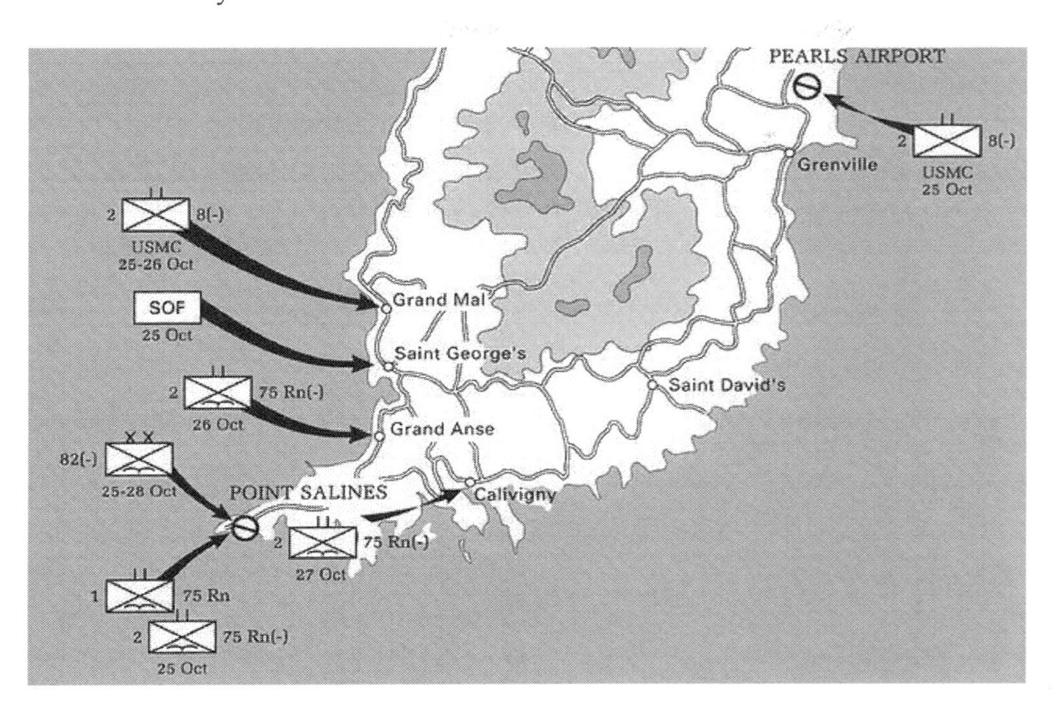

One group of SEALs was tasked with capturing the island radio tower.

They got surrounded in the radio tower by Cuban backed communists in armored cars. A firefight ensued! Heavily outgunned and outnumbered the Navy SEALs held their own, and staved off the communist rebels.

Murphy's law visited them (there he is again!); their walkie-talkie batteries had been run down, and they had no communication with their base!

After much improvisation, and cursing, they avoided disaster by using a normal telephone to call in backup.

They destroyed the tower in the fight to get out, and made their way to the water where they swam to the open sea.

They had to swim along the coast of Grenada for SIX hours!

Finally they were extracted by a reconnaissance plane.

Meanwhile, another SEAL Team was busy freeing Governor General Scoon who was trapped in his mansion. The SEALs entered the mansion with little resistance, but, this time the communist forces were already aware of the invasion.

They surrounded the Governor's mansion with armored cars and BTR-60 eight wheeled tanks and started a counter attack!

The SEALs were trapped for 24 hours until Marines from the 250 "G" Company came with their amphibious assault vehicles and four M60 Patton tanks.

They destroyed the communist forces and their BTR-60's and relieved the Navy SEALs the next morning.

Governor Scoon, his wife, and nine others were safely evacuated the same day.

The fighting of Operation Urgent Fury was over in THREE days.

Army Rangers and United States Marines secured the island and freed the American university students.

In the aftermath, it was found that the Soviet Union and Cuba were much more heavily involved than we thought:

Enemy forces casualties and losses

Grenada:
45 killed
337 wounded
6 APCs destroyed
1 armoured car destroyed

Cuba:
25 killed
59 wounded
638 captured
2 transport aircraft captured

Soviet Union:
2 wounded
Weapons cache seized:
12 APCs
12 anti-aircraft guns
291 submachine guns
6,330 rifles
5.6 million rounds of ammunition

American casualties and losses

19 killed

116 wounded

9 helicopters lost

Operation Red Wings - The Battle of Abbas Ghar

Operation red wings will go down in Navy SEALs infamy.

This is one mission that didn't go too well.

The Navy SEALs were tasked with capturing a high-ranking Taliban leader in the Kumar province of Afghanistan.

This *was* the plan:

- **Phase 1: Shaping:** A U.S. Navy SEAL reconnaissance and surveillance team is tasked to insert in the region of the suspected safe buildings of Ahmad Shah, observe and identify Shah and his men and specific locations, and guide a direct action team of phase two to structures in which Shah and his men are observed to be staying.
- **Phase 2:** Action on the Objective: A SEAL direct action team is to be inserted by MH-47, followed shortly by Marines, to capture or kill Shah and his men.
- **Phase 3:** Outer Cordon: Marines, along with Afghan National Army soldiers, are to sweep surrounding valleys for other suspected insurgents.
- **Phase 4:** Security and Stabilization: In the days after the first three phases, U.S. Marines and Afghan National Army soldiers and U.S. Navy corpsmen will provide medical care to the local population and determine local needs, such as improved roads, wells, and schools.
- **Phase 5:** Exfiltration: Depending on enemy activity, the Marines will remain in the area for up to one month, then depart the area.

And *this* is what happened:

On the night of June 27, 2005, the Night Stalkers were tasked with inserting the reconnaissance team of four Navy SEALs.

Night Stalkers: The Army's Special Operations Command's 160th Special Operations Aviation Regiment (SOAR).

They flew in two MH-47 Chinook helicopters. One flew as a decoy around the mountain tops and performed "decoy drops" to confuse the enemy, while the other Chinook hovered at a point between Sawtalo Sar and Gatigal Sar, a peak just to the south of Sawtalo Sar:

Fly to it in Google Earth!

The Four SEALs then fast roped down and...

All hell broke loose...

Once they were on the ground, they immediately ran into some local goat herders. The SEAL team determined that they were not enemy combatants, or Taliban, so they let them go.

This proved to be a BIG mistake.

The Taliban fighters commanded by Ahmad Shah were waiting in ambush. Once the goat herders went back to their village, the fighters attacked with AK-47's, RPG's, RPK machine guns, and an 82mm mortar!

Three of the four SEALs were killed, and the fourth, Petty Officer Marcus Luttrell, was left unconscious and wounded.

Then things got worse.

> *When things can go wrong, they will go wrong, and at the worst possible moment.--Murphy's Law*

During the attack, the SEAL team leader was able to make contact with home base. The commanding officer launched a rescue mission immediately.

Now operation Red Wings 2 started!

A Quick Reaction Force (QRF) was assembled with Army Rangers, SEAL Team 10, and a whole slew of Army 160th Night Stalkers awesomeness: two MH-47 Chinooks, two UH-60 Black Hawks, and two AH-64 Apaches.

However, the Taliban fighters were still waiting there in the valley!

Once the rescue team arrived, the enemy fighters shot down the lead MH-47 Chinook with RPG's (Rocket Propelled Grenades):

RPG-7

RPK machine gun

Eight soldiers of the army's 160th Special Forces operation regiment SOR deployed to rescue the SEAL team. They all died in the helicopter crash, along with eight SEALs from Team 10 that were with them.

This is the actual hand drawn map the Navy SEALs used in Operation Red Wings:

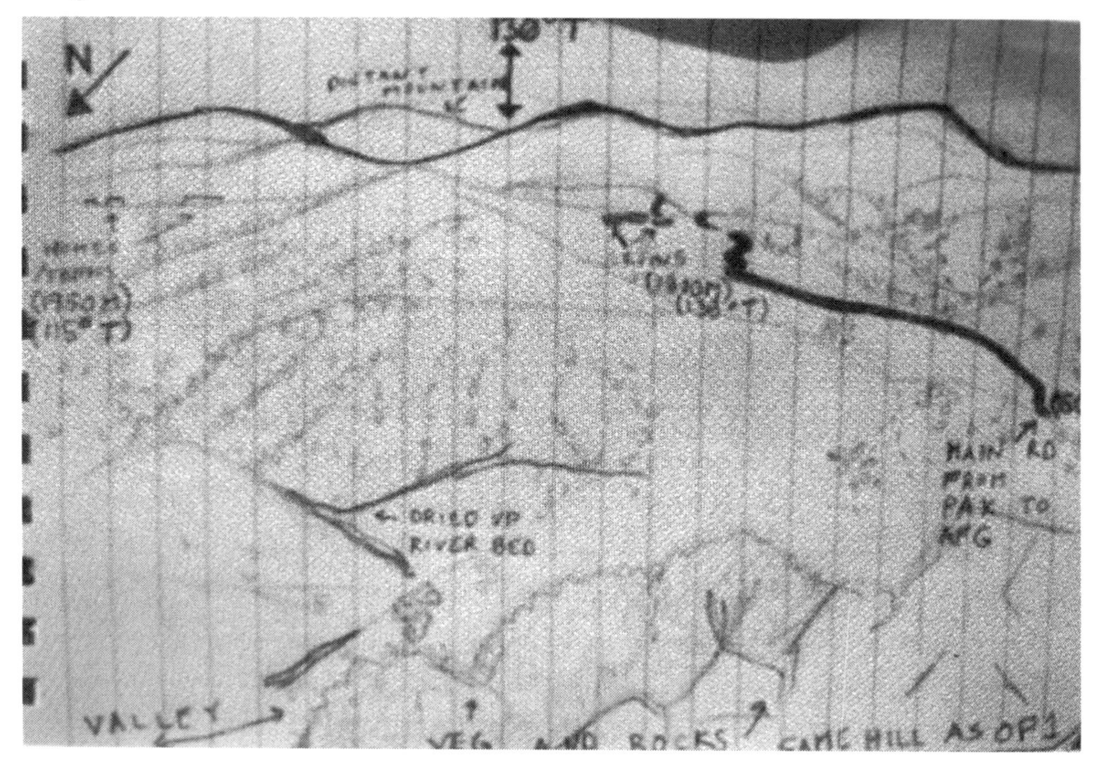

AK-47:

There was a silver lining however.

Marcus Luttrell, the only survivor, managed to get himself to a village—despite his fractured neck and leg! Luckily the village, Salar Ban in the Shuryek valley, was pro-American.

An elderly man in the village actually protected him from further Taliban assaults. The Pashtun people of Afghanistan are very traditional and honor "Pashtunwali," the custom of giving a stranger who enters your village asylum (Nanawatai) to protect him from his enemies. He refused to give-up Marcus Lutrell to the Taliban!

Help was on the way...

A massive search began with Army Rangers and pararescuemen (also called PJ's) of the U.S. Air Force.

It took five days to rescue Lutrell who was effectively paralyzed from the waist down by ELEVEN gunshot wounds.

The battle was later called "the worst single day loss of life for Naval Special Warfare personnel since World War II."*

(You can read more about Marcus Luttrell's journey in his book "Lone Survivor". See the recommended reading section in the back of this book.)

**Unfortunately this record has been surpassed by the August 2011 shoot-down and crash of an MH-47 Chinook helicopter carrying over 30 special forces and US military personnel over the Tangi Valley in Maidan Wardak province, southwest of Kabul, Afghanistan.*

Captain Phillips 2009: Maersk Alabama

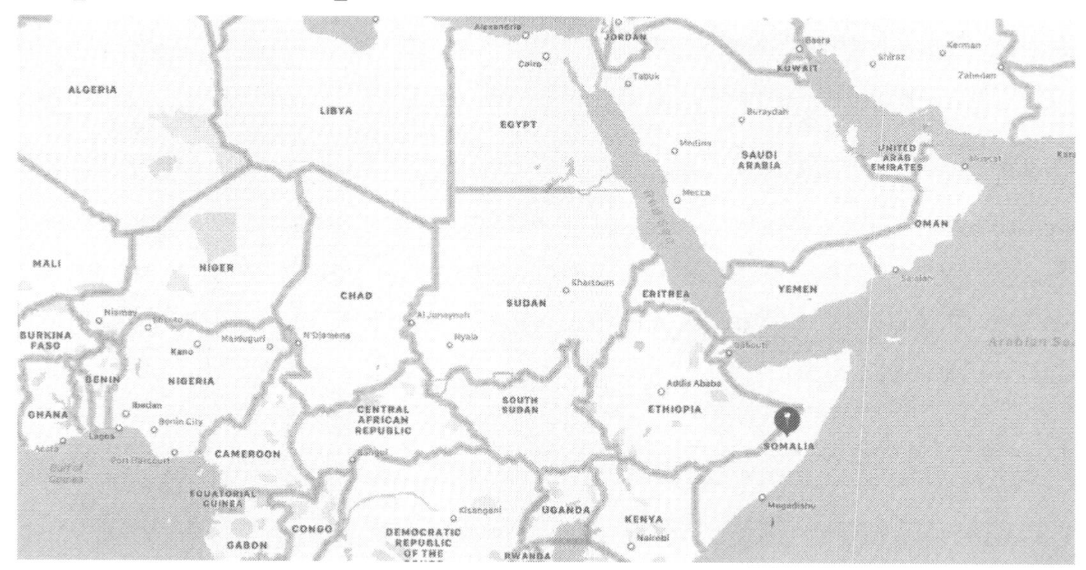

Perhaps one of the more famous Navy SEALs interventions was the rescue of Captain Phillips.

In 2009 Somali pirates took his ship hostage; the Maersk Alabama:

Did you know that big ships are actually very easy to capture? They have no guns to defend themselves! So the Somali pirates just come up in a little boat, and board the ship. Can't get simpler than that!

However, Captain Phillip's crew did not give up without a fight!

After the pirates boarded his ship...

Captain Phillips cut the power and the entire ship went black—no lights.

In the darkness of the engine room, the Chief Engineer Mike Perry was waiting for the pirates with his hunting knife.

Without night-vision goggles, the crew and the pirates hunted each other in the darkness below!—he was able to catch one of the pirates!

At the same time, some of the other pirates on board were able to capture Captain Phillips.

After negotiating with some of the pirates, Chief Engineer Perry was able to regain control of the Maersk Alabama, but the other four pirates escaped with Captain Phillips on a lifeboat.

At this time the Maersk Alabama was sailing to port Mombasa Kenya, but the lifeboat was drifting helplessly at sea with Captain Phillips and the four pirates.

This gave the Navy a strategic window to act...

The USS Bainbridge was the closest ship, but they didn't have any Navy SEALs on board. What do you do when you are at sea and need the Navy SEALs?

Of course!—you parachute them in!

On Sunday, 12 April 2009, SEAL Team 6 Snipers of Naval Special Warfare Development Group (DEVGRU) "Red Squadron" parachuted in and landed IN THE SEA next to the USS Bainbridge. If you look closely, you can see their swimming-fins on their feet:

They quickly set-up at strategic positions on the ship's stern. The crew had been monitoring the pirates with a ScanEagle; a small, long-endurance, low-altitude Unmanned Aerial Vehicle (UAV):

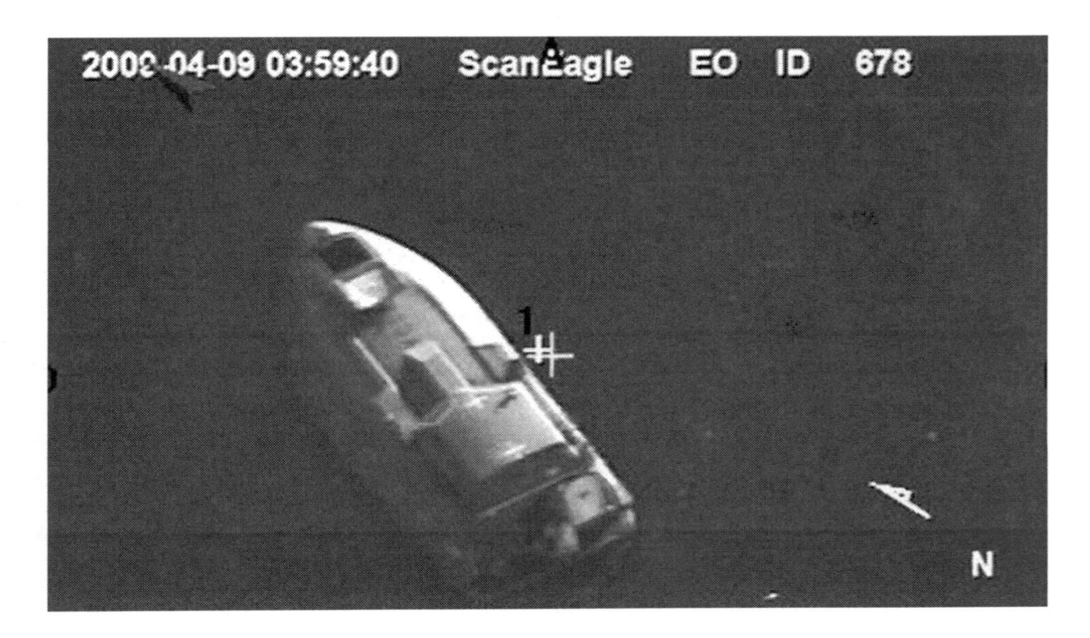

It looked like the Pirates were about to shoot Captain Phillips!

However...

...they did not reckon with the Navy SEAL snipers!

The mood was TENSE, the winds were whipping up, the waves in the sea were bouncing the lifeboat, a real NIGHTMARE for a sniper who needs a steady target and a guaranteed "One-Shot-One-Kill!

Despite all of the challenges, the three Navy snipers zeroed in on the pirates in the bobbing boat—all three snipers pulled their triggers SIMULTANEOUSLY and killed the three Somali pirates instantly!

Let's hear It for the Navy SEALs snipers!

Operation Neptune Spear: The Raid on Osama bin Laden 2011

By far, the most famous Navy Seals mission was the mission to get Osama bin Laden, the leader of the Al-Qaeda, and the terrorist who led the September 11 attacks on the United States which killed over 3,000 people.

The terrorist Mastermind had been hiding in Abbottabad Pakistan for years.

Osama Bin Laden's Compound in Abbottabad:

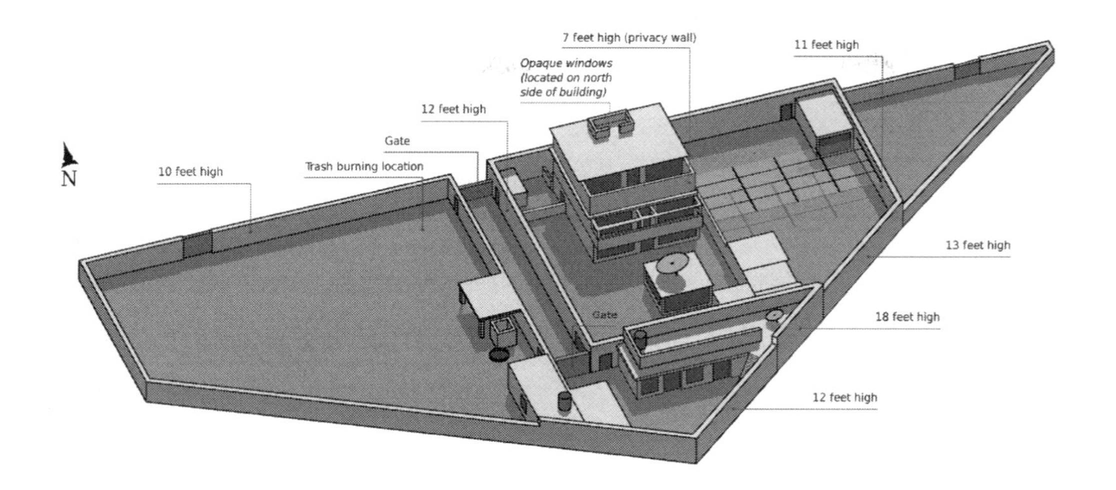

Indeed his compound was so big, it's hard to believe that he could hide there in plain view, right in the middle of a large city. It is suspected that the government of Pakistan was shielding him.

Nevertheless, Osama Bin Laden practiced a very strict security regime.

The United States has the best SIGINT (Signals Intelligence) capabilities in the world. So if you use an electronic device, like a smartphone, or satellite phone, the SIGINT departments of the U.S. military will pick it up, and LOCATE you.

Previous accomplices of Osama Bin Laden, who had used satellite telephones were quickly located, and killed by the US special forces.

After this, Osama Bin Laden removed the internet connections in his entire compound, and any communications with his subordinates or other leaders were conducted by USB stick.

That's correct; he had messengers carry a USB stick with videos and text messages from him on it, and actually hand deliver the messages to his leaders and subordinates. Just like in the old days before telephones existed.

And vice versa; the leaders and subordinates would answer him and communicate with him also through a USB stick.
This is the only communication method that is relatively safe. It made it impossible for any of the United States intelligence agencies to intercept his messages; like email, telephone, or satellite-telephone, or even internet communications—because he had none!

Indeed the only way to have 100% secure communications today is by directly hand delivering your messages yourself.
So how did they find him?

This remains a secret to this day. However, we do know that someone observed Osama Bin Laden's messenger coming and going with the USB sticks and communications on them.

Several agencies came together like the U.S. Navy and the CIA to form a plan of attack, and the final decision to *GO* was made by president Obama.

Operation Neptune Spear was actually coordinated by the CIA, so technically the SEALs were CIA operatives—and civilians—for this short time.

This was an important point for the politics of the situation. The CIA is a civilian organization, therefore the Navy SEALs chosen for this mission were technically "private contractors" and not American military members.

Why is this important?

If the mission would have gone wrong, or the Navy Seals been caught, President Obama could have said, "We did not conduct any *military* operations in Pakistan." Because the United States was negotiating with Pakistan, and at the time was actually friends with Pakistan—and you don't conduct military operations against your friends.

SEAL Team 6 was chosen for the task!

On May 2nd 2011 before dawn, two U.S. Army helicopters of the 160th Special Operations Aviation Regiment (SOAR)—also known as "Night Stalkers" flew the Navy SEALs to Osama bin Laden's compound in top secret STEALTH HELICOPTERS.

Among them they also had a Malinois combat dog!

As they approached the compound, one of the helicopters brushed the wall with its tail rotor and crashed. Luckily no one was injured.

The Navy SEALs had to destroy the helicopter with explosives so that nobody could use, or reverse engineer the stealth technology—it's top secret!

Then the Navy SEALs went straight to their job: they used explosives to blow up the gates. The first gate they blew-up was a fake. It was just doors installed on a solid wall. So when they blew it up, the doors flew off but the wall was still there!

They tried another door on the other side of the compound. They blew the doors off, and entered the compound.

Once inside they cleared the floors one by one, working their way up to the top floor.

They met resistance, however, the fighters inside the compound were no match for the Navy SEALS. With the power lines cut and no light inside, everyone was operating in the pitch black of night.

Everyone that is, except the SEALs! They had night-vision goggles, and quickly dispatched the enemy terrorists in the compound.

After clearing the first and second floors, the SEALs made it to the third floor where they found Osama bin Laden. We will never know the exact details, but the best information shows that he had one of his wives in front of him, using her as a shield, and an AK-47 in the other hand, ready and pointing at the door as the lead SEAL came in.

The human shield technique did not work, and the Navy SEAL quickly dispatched Osama bin Laden.

The entire operation took less than 40 minutes, and the United States had finally gotten the #1 terrorist mastermind after a 10-year manhunt.

Since they didn't have any photographs on hand or other means to identify Osama bin Laden, they used his height as an indicator. They knew that he was about 6 feet 4 inches tall. So they had one of the Navy SEALs who was also 6 feet tall lay down right next to Osama bin Laden's body, to see how tall he was.

Later, the CIA and U.S. special forces performed more rigorous photo identification and DNA analysis to positively identify him as Osama bin Laden.

Watch the interview with the Navy SEAL who got Osama bin Laden here!

What is Leadership?

Leadership is lonely.

You'll be surprised at how many of your friends turn out to *not* be friends after you become a leader.

☆☆☆☆☆

Leadership Hurts.

You will have to make decisions that make you unpopular.

You're going to have to do things that nobody else will do.

That's what makes you a leader!

☆☆☆☆☆

Leadership is an experience, and LIFE-long learning:

And no matter how painful or lonely it is at the top—it is worth it!

Do you want to be the person **taking** orders or **giving** orders?

Do you want to be constantly griping about how to do things right, or be the one making the decisions?—well then, step up to the plate!

That's the difference: the leaders stepped up to the plate and took the job.

If there is one thing I have learned, do not shun leadership positions!

Go towards them, take them no matter how painful or lonely they are.

It is worth it, because then YOU are the leader, making the decisions.

Be the person that YOU want to be.

Don't be the follower.

☆☆☆☆☆

There are many answers to this question, but let's take the answer directly from a famous Navy SEAL: Jocko Willink.

In true Navy SEALs fashion, he has boiled the leadership question down to two simple but super EFFECTIVE Words:

Extreme ownership!

"Extreme Ownership" is the only way to go!

When you own your mistakes, you are on the path to leadership.

Additionally, even if you are not in a leadership position, owning your mistakes is the ONLY way to a solution.

Book Bonuses!

An interview with a real Navy SEAL

Stew Smith is a Navy SEAL and fitness expert.

He runs fitness challenges and fitness programs to get people ready for the armed forces and Navy SEALs.

I had the pleasure of interviewing Stew on the KidsBooks.Club website here:

He will get you ready to pass the physical tests!

Recommended Reading

These are the recommended leadership books for anybody that wants to become a Navy SEAL.

You can find this list on the **KidsBooks.Club** website, consider them mandatory reading:

#1 The Operator, recently published by Robert O'neill, The Navy SEAL **who got Osama Bin Laden**, and was on Captain Phillips rescue!

This book is a GREAT read that takes you from the very beginning, from training for the Navy SEALs physical tests and BUD/S—to going all the way to the battle field, in the most SECRET and ELITE special operations ever...*ever!*

Kids will definitely appreciate his detailed account of BUD/S!

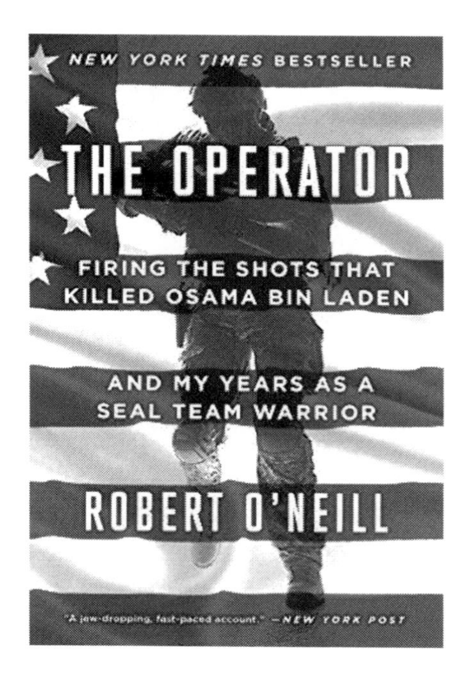

#2 Rogue Warrior by Dick Marcinko

Wow! What a book!

If "The Operator" got you fired up - you GOTTA read this book.

You will be hooked and binge read the entire series!

Dick Marcinko— **founder of SEAL Team 6**— takes you from UDT training, SEAL Team 2, Viet Nam, Cambodia, Beirut and more!

You will love his choice of words!

☆☆☆☆☆

#3 Extreme Ownership by Jocko Willink and Leif Babin. This is definitely the number one leadership book; written by real Navy SEALs!

The lesson of this book is profound, and extreme, and simple. That's the best thing about this book: to distill leadership down to 2 words, "extreme ownership", is not only amazing, but super helpful; mandatory Reading!

☆☆☆☆☆

#4 Lone Survivor by Marcus Luttrell.

This is the story of Operation Redwings by Marcus Luttrell, the ONLY one who survived the attack on that fateful day in Afghanistan!

Required reading!

☆☆☆☆☆

#5 The Power of Positive Thinking by Norman Vincent Peale.

This is the book that started it all:

All of those mindset and success books out there today are all based on this book.

Mindset is everything. And it starts with believing in yourself, and having a tenacity to never give up (exactly like the Navy SEALs!) and by the way, if you don't think this works, guess what President Trump read when he was a kid? Guess Who his pastor was when he went to church? —Norman Vincent Peale, the author of this book!

☆☆☆☆☆

#5 Think and Grow Rich by Napoleon Hill.

This book is actually older than the power of positive thinking from Norman Vincent Peale but no less powerful.

It's not really about money. I don't know why Napoleon Hill named it that, but he shouldn't have. A better name would have been "how to be successful and develop persistence and tenacity."

You should DO this book backwards: read the chapter about fear first, then start at the beginning and make your master plan.

It is important that you write down your master plan.

And, you will be amazed at how well it works! You can always come back to your master plan in times of need, to get back on track. This book not only covers the mindset (like Norman Vincent Peale's) but also goes a little bit deeper into how to realize your goals and be successful. *Pure awesomeness!*

#6 About Face by Colonel David H. Hackworth.

This is an amazing book about the rigors, and horrors of war, and the leadership lessons that you MUST learn the hard way.

This book is profound on many levels and is mandatory reading not only for Navy SEALs, but for all soldiers, and people going to war.

Because of this, it is actually good for anybody, anywhere, anytime—a real life lessons book...amazing!

Check out all of the books HERE!

Link List

Dear Reader,

The following list contains "bitlinks". That means all you have to do is type in any internet browser "bit.ly/___" and your browser will take you there! No need for "http.." or "www"! But you do have to type them in EXACTLY, paying special attention to small letters or CaPitaL letters too:

Which Special Forces are YOU? Quiz — bit.ly/specForces
Video: Why a guaranteed job is so important — bit.ly/32JTkM2
Admiral McRaven's speech — bit.ly/2U4bllY
Room Clearing Exercise with a quadcopter — bit.ly/2J2IHv5
Navy SEALs SERE Training — bit.ly/33ARvSu
Video: Navy SEALs ship boarding mission — bit.ly/2WG6GIz
Navy SEALs martial arts! — bit.ly/2UeRu3I
Download the complete MCMAP —bit.ly/2QCT6lB
HALO infographic https — bit.ly/2J7nEYf
The difference between the others, AMAZING vid! — bit.ly/3blPOee
Watch the SWCC deploy their speed boats — bit.ly/33TPbWY
SWCC a real HOT extract! — bit.ly/3amIOxx
The Navy's Marine Mammal Program — bit.ly/3bpcj23
Combat Dog Takedown! — bit.ly/combatdog
Operation Red Wings Insertion Point — bit.ly/2QQCpmv
Interview with the Navy SEAL who got 'bin Laden — bit.ly/RobertOneill
Interview with Stew Smith: SEAL's fitness expert! — bit.ly/InterviewStew
Recommended Reading List — bit.ly/RECOMMENDED-READING

Dear Reader,
I hope you enjoyed this book! If you don't mind, REVIEWS are the life's-blood of every author.

It would mean the world to me if you would leave a review for this book on Amazon :-)

Please review this book on Amazon!

Do you like FREE books?

There are a bunch of them on the KidsBooks.Club! Here are just a few, scan the codes below and get them—they're free!

Made in United States
Orlando, FL
03 December 2024